HOCKEY SOUPS

HOCKEY SOUPS

Soup Recipes from Around the World

BY THE MEMBER NATIONAL ASSOCIATIONS OF THE INTERNATIONAL ICE HOCKEY FEDERATION

FOREWORDS BY GARY BETTMAN & JACQUES ROGGE

Fenn Publishing Company Ltd.
Bolton, Ontario, Canada

INTERNATIONAL
ICE HOCKEY
FEDERATION

IMPRESSUM

Idea & concept	Horst Lichtner
Authors	Lucas Rosenblatt & Horst Lichtner, Lucerne
Layout & design	Stephanie Rosenblatt, Basel
Photos	Jules Moser, Berne
Editors	Dr. Katharina Lichtner, Heidi Blättler, Lucerne
Hockey text	Szymon Szemberg, Zurich
Translations	Anton & Jacqueline Güggi, Meggen
Support	Roman Stübinger, Lucerne
Dishes	Globus Lucerne & Cascade Lucerne
Publisher	Jordan Fenn, Key Porter Books, Toronto

HOCKEY SOUPS
A Fenn Publishing Book / First Published in 2010

All rights reserved

Copyright 2010 © International Ice Hockey Federation.

No part of the work covered by the copyrights herein may be reproduced or used in any form or by any means – graphic, electronic or mechanical, including photocopying, recording, taping or information storage and retrieval systems – without the prior written permission of the publisher, or, in case of photocopying or other reprographic copying, a license from Access Copyright, the Canadian Copyright Licensing Agency, One Yonge Street, Suite 1900, Toronto, Ontario, M6B 3A9.

The content, opinion and subject matter contained herein is the written expression of the author and does not reflect the opinion or ideology of the publisher, or that of the publisher's representatives.

Fenn Publishing Company Ltd.
Bolton, Ontario, Canada
www.hbfenn.com

The publisher gratefully acknowledges the support of the Canada Council for the Arts and the Ontario Arts Council for its publishing program. We acknowledge the support of the Government of Ontario through the Ontario Media Development Corporation's Ontario Book Initiative.

We acknowledge the financial support of the Government of Canada through the Book Publishing Industry Development Program (BPIDP) for our publishing activities. Care has been taken to trace ownership of copyright material in this book and to secure permissions. The publishers will gladly receive any information that will enable them to rectify errors or omissions.

Printed and bound in Canada

Library and Archives Canada Cataloguing in Publication

    Hockey soups : soup recipes from around the world / International Ice
Hockey Federation ; foreword by Gary Bettman & Jacques Rogge.

ISBN 978-1-55168-343-0 (bound)

    1. Soups. 2. Hockey--History. 3. Hockey teams.
I. International Ice Hockey Federation

TX757.H595 2010   641.8'13   C2009-907033-2

DEDICATED TO
RENÉ FASEL
IIHF PRESIDENT

INTERNATIONAL
OLYMPIC
COMMITTEE

JACQUES ROGGE

Dear ice hockey fans and soup lovers,

As the President of the International Olympic Committee it is a great pleasure for me to contribute with a foreword to this book. It doesn't happen very often in the world of sports, where so much is written and communicated, that an initiative from one of our International Member Federations presents this unique combination of sports and gastronomy.

The 2010 Olympic Winter Games in Vancouver, Canada, provide us with the opportunity to come to the motherland of ice hockey. One can feel the excitement over this event throughout this enormous country. Therefore I am convinced that fans in Canada, and in other countries, will find this book inspiring, both from the parts about sport, but especially from the soup recipes from the different countries.

Sixty national member associations of the IIHF have contributed to this book. It is just another wonderful display of the possibilities of international sports to exceed borders and to work together to accomplish something entirely new.

I wish the International Ice Hockey Federation all the best in the future and I hope that this book will be well received by fans, players and officials. And of course, I wish the IIHF President a happy 60th birthday and lots of joy with cooking of the soups in the upcoming years.

Jacques Rogge
IOC President

GARY BETTMAN

Dear hockey friends,

The NHL is proud that so many players from so many different nations are taking part in the 2010 Olympic Winter Games in Vancouver. The best players in the world will compete for the Olympic title and many fans from all over the world are waiting with great anticipation for this amazing event in Canada.

This book, with more than 60 soups from 60 countries, is an initiative of the IIHF on the occasion of the exciting Olympic Games that the world awaits. It also is in honour of the 60th birthday of a man that I have come to know and respect over the past 15 years, IIHF President René Fasel. Without the determination of René, and the good cooperation between the NHL and the IIHF, we would not be in Vancouver to watch best-on-best Olympic hockey.

It is with great pleasure that I wish René a happy 60th birthday. I know that all the people who will enjoy this book will join me in my well wishes for both a happy birthday and a great Olympic Winter Games!

Gary Bettman
NHL Commissioner

René Fasel, President of the International Ice Hockey Federation, celebrates his 60th birthday during the 2010 Olympic Winter Games in Vancouver. We have enjoyed cooking and eating for many years with our *Schlemmerclub* in Lucerne and this is how and where we came across the idea of this book. Now, in honour of René's birthday and in recognition of his passionate love of soups, we offer this book of the most popular soup recipes from the countries of the IIHF member associations.

For the last two years we have collected recipes and have researched, cooked, tasted and photographed the results, with the invaluable assistance of many to whom we owe our warm gratitude. First, we thank all the member associations who helped us find the appropriate recipes. Special thanks go to Nicole Bosshardt and to Kristina Koch who worked tirelessly to sort, compile, and organize the recipes; and to Dr. Katharina Lichtner and Heidi Blättler, who spent many weekends translating and editing them after demanding weeks at work. Heartfelt thanks go also to photographer Jules Moser and to his assistant Lea Hunziker for their professional expertise. It was a joy to assemble, illustrate, and present these outstanding recipes. We thank last but not least our many ice hockey colleagues in Canada who enthusiastically encouraged and promoted this project.

To all our readers and cooks we wish success and fun in discovering the delectable wide world of soups.

HORST LICHTNER AND LUCAS ROSENBLATT

Horst Lichtner and Lucas Rosenblatt

TABLE OF CONTENTS

LEGEND

All data as of 2009

Participation

WM	IIHF World Championship
WM I	IIHF World Championship, Division I
WM II	IIHF World Championship, Division II
WM III	IIHF World Championship, Division III
WW	IIHF World Women Championship
WW I	IIHF World Women Championship, Division I
WW II	IIHF World Women Championship, Division II
WW18	IIHF World Women U18 Championship
WW18 I	IIHF World Women U18 Championship, Division I
WM20	IIHF World U20 Championship
WM20 I	IIHF World U20 Championship, Division I
WM20 II	IIHF World U20 Championship, Division II
WM20 III	IIHF World U20 Championship, Division III
WM18	IIHF World U18 Championship
WM18 I	IIHF World U18 Championship, Division I
WM18 II	IIHF World U18 Championship, Division II
WM18 III	IIHF World U18 Championship, Division III

Population

Source: CIA World Factbook

UNITS

Liquid measures

tsp.	Teaspoon (about 5 ml)
tbsp.	Tablespoon (about 15 ml)
c.	Cup (about 250 ml)
pt.	Pint (about 500 ml)
qt.	Quart (about 1 litre)

Dry measures

pn.	Pinch (less than ½ g)
oz.	Ounce (about 30 g)
lb.	Pound (about 500 g)
bn.	Bunch / Bundle (e.g. herbs)

All recipes serve 4 people.

ANDORRA

ANDORRA'S HOCKEY HISTORY

Ice hockey did not begin in Andorra until the 1990s. Lack of ice (one indoor rink) and equipment slowed the development of the game. There are around 90 players in the small country. A major step towards popularizing the sport was made when the country joined the IIHF in 1995 and hosted the «D» Pool World Championship in 1996–97 in Canillo. Teams from Andorra currently play exhibition games only.

ICE HOCKEY IN ANDORRA

Federation

Registered Players:	71
Senior:	29
Juvenile:	42
Female:	15

Referees

Male:	0
Female:	1

Rinks

Indoor:	1
Outdoor:	0

Participation	-
Population	83,888

3 c. broth

7 oz. onion (cut in rings)

3½ oz. Gruyere cheese (Swiss hard cheese, grated)

4 eggs* (only yolks)

4 slices of toast

Butter and oil

*Eggs are separated just before putting them into the individual soup bowls. The egg yolk is carefully dropped into the soup so that it remains whole.

With a little oil and some butter, stir-fry the onion until golden. Set aside.

Take 4 earthenware bowls and spread the onion. Bring the broth to a boil and evenly share into the bowls. Now add 1 egg yolk. Shape the toast in the form of the bowl (round) and place on top of the soup. Sprinkle the grated cheese over the toast and bake in a preheated oven at 220°C / 430°F for 5 minutes. Serve immediately.

ONION SOUP

ARMENIA'S HOCKEY HISTORY

The town of Svedlosvsk (now Jekaterinburg), Russia hosted a tournament that pitted all of the Soviet States against one another in 1962. The Armenians participated and lost, 1–0, to Lithuania. Years later, Armenia, has returned to the hockey world. It joined the IIHF in 2000. Armenia made its international debut in 2004 when it took part in Division III of the World Championship. The first Armenian hockey championship took place in 2001 and was won by ASC Erevan.

ICE HOCKEY IN ARMENIA

Federation

Registered Players:	578
Senior:	381
Juvenile:	197
Female:	0

Referees

Male:	27
Female:	0

Rinks

Indoor:	2
Outdoor:	3

Participation   -

Population   2,967,004

ARMENIA

1-2 potatoes

1 small onion (finely chopped)

1 cabbage leaf (finely chopped)

1 stalk celery (finely chopped)

4-5 green beans (finely chopped)

1 carrot (in small cubes)

2 green chili (finely chopped)

3½ oz. peas

¼ c. tomato juice

2 c. chicken broth

5 oz. beef cubed

2 oz. egg noodles (optional)

Garnish

1 tbsp. parsley

Clean and dice all the vegetables and drain. Bring the chicken broth and the tomato juice to a boil, and then add vegetables, the meat and egg noodles (if desired). Cook for ½ hour and serve garnished with parsley.

BOZBASH
WITH CHICKEN

AUSTRALIA'S HOCKEY HISTORY

The first hockey game played in Australia was in 1907 when a group of Melbourne skaters challenged the crew of the American battleship, *Baltimore*. Although the home team was defeated, the groundwork for the future development of the sport was laid. Australia joined the IIHF in 1950, though the Federation was not founded until 1954. The world caught its first glimpse of the Australian national team at the 1960 Olympics. The Aussies lost all six matches by an aggregate score of 88–10. In 2009, Australia scored its biggest success with the promotion to Division I.

AUSTRALIA

ICE HOCKEY IN AUSTRALIA

Federation

Registered Players:	2836
Senior:	1805
Juvenile:	816
Female:	215

Referees

Male:	231
Female:	29

Rinks

Indoor:	20
Outdoor:	0

Participation
WM I, WM20 III, WM18 III

Population	21,262,641

3 c. good-quality chicken stock

1 c. water

2 lbs. butternut pumpkin
(peeled, roughly chopped)

1 large onion (roughly chopped)

2 carrots (roughly chopped)

3 celery sticks (roughly chopped)

2 cloves of garlic

1 tsp. paprika

½ tsp. turmeric

½ tsp. ground coriander

½ tsp. ground nutmeg

Garnish

4 tbsp. pumpkin seeds
(roasted, chopped)

1 bn. coriander leaves

In a large saucepan, bring chicken stock and water to a boil. Add the vegetables and spices and heat until boiling. Reduce heat and simmer for 20 minutes, or until vegetables are soft. Allow to cool and then pureé using a blender or hand-held processor. Season to taste. Reheat soup and serve it garnished with coriander and pumpkin seeds.

BUTTERNUT PUMPKIN SOUP

ICE HOCKEY IN AUSTRIA

Federation

Registered Players:	10378
Senior:	4631
Juvenile:	5109
Female:	638

Referees

Male:	257
Female:	12

Rinks

Indoor:	25
Outdoor:	106

Participation

WM, WW I, W20 I, WM18 I, WW18 I

Population	8,205,533

AUSTRIA

AUSTRIA'S HOCKEY HISTORY

Austrian hockey received a boost when the first artificial ice rink opened in Vienna in 1909. The Austrian Hockey Union was created in 1912, and was admitted to the IIHF two months later. Austria played its first international game on February 2, 1912, losing 5–0 to Bohemia. Austria won the 1927 and 1931 European Championships. Austria spent most of the 60s competing in the «B» Pool but began to alternate with «C» Pool. Improved results occurred in the 80s and they qualified for the Olympics 1984, 1988 and 1998. Austria is currently ranked 16th in the world, switching between the top Division and Division I.

2 lbs. beef bones with meat

2 carrots

1 celery root

1 leek

1 clove garlic

Nutmeg

Salt and pepper

1 bn. chives

For the fritatten

1 egg

1 oz. wheat flour

2½ oz. whole milk

1 tbsp. butter (melted)

1bn. parsley (finely chopped)

Nutmeg

1 pn. salt

Stock

Put beef bones into a stock pot and fill with 2½ quarts of water. Cut vegetables into big chunks and add to soup. Season with salt, pepper and nutmeg. Cook the stock for 1½ hours. Strain soup and set the stock aside.

Fritatten

Mix the egg with the salt and nutmeg. While sieving through a colander, slowly add the flour to the mixture, continuously stirring to ensure smooth dough. Keep on stirring and slowly add the milk. Put a lid on the dough and set aside for 20 minutes. Stir butter and parsley into the dough and fry in a non-stick frying pan to pancakes (crêpes). Let them cool and then cut into ½-inch wide strips.

Bring stock to a quick boil. Carefully add the fritatten into the simmering stock. Let simmer for approximately 5 minutes. Garnish with some chives prior to serving.

CLASSIC VIENNESE BEEF SOUP
WITH FRITATTEN

BELARUS

BELARUS' HOCKEY HISTORY

Hockey in the Belarus became popular after World War II. Belarus became a member of the IIHF on May 6, 1992, and staged its first national championship in 1992–93. Dynamo Minsk won and finished 10th in the KHL of the Commonwealth of Independent States. Belarus debuted its national team in 1992 hosting a qualification tournament for the 1993 «C» Pool. Belarus rose to the «A» Pool in 1998. The 1998 Nagano Olympics saw Belarus win their Preliminary Round group. The country has developed many excellent young players in recent years and they are ranked 7th in the world.

ICE HOCKEY IN BELARUS

Federation
Registered Players:	3302
Senior:	1000
Juvenile:	2300
Female:	2

Referees
Male:	109
Female:	0

Rinks
Indoor:	19
Outdoor:	3

Participation
WM, WM20 I, WM18 I

Population 9,648,533

БЕЛАРУСЬ

2 c. beef stock

8 oz. beef cubes

1½ cups sauerkraut

2 oz. white mushrooms (quartered)

2 oz. carrots (finely chopped)

2 oz. onion (finely chopped)

1 tsp. tomato paste

4 tbsp. oil

2 tbsp. flour

2 cloves garlic

2 bay leaf

Salt and pepper

1 tbsp. butter

½ lb. puff pastry
(in four portions to cover soup bowls)

Sour cream (as a side dish)

Heat the oil in a large pan and fry the onions and the carrots, remove and set aside. Add sauerkraut, beef and the tomato paste to the same pan and stew with the lid on. Return the fried carrot and onion and stirring occasionally, continue to cook over low heat for 20 minutes or until softened. Add the stock and let it simmer for 30 minutes. Remove two ladles of liquid and set aside to cool. In a separate pan heat the butter; add the flour and heat until golden brown (stirring continuously). Pour the cooled liquid into the browned flour stir making sure no lumps of flour remain. Add mixture to the remaindar of the soup and season with salt and spices.

Let the soup cool and ladle the soup evenly into small earthenware pots, add the mushrooms and cover the pot with puff pastry. Put the soup into the oven for 15-20 minutes. The sour cream is served separately. The temperature of the soup is to be not less than 75°C.

SHCHI
WITH MUSHROOMS AND CRACKLE BUN IN A POT STEWED IN OVEN

BELGIUM

BELGIUM'S HOCKEY HISTORY

In 1908, the Royal Belgian Ice Hockey Federation was founded. The Belgians were active during the early days of ice hockey. Belgium joined France, Bohemia, England, and Switzerland as the fifth member of the IIHF. The first national championship was held in 1912. At the first European Championship in 1910, Belgium earned the bronze and then won the European title in 1913. Since 1987, the Belgians have participated at either the «C» or «D» Pool World Championship. Paul Loicq, who was president of the IIHF for 25 years, is the most famous Belgian in the history of international hockey.

ICE HOCKEY IN BELGIUM

Federation

Registered Players:	1192
Senior:	356
Juvenile:	753
Female:	83

Referees

Male:	35
Female:	6

Rinks

Indoor:	12
Outdoor:	1

Participation
WM II, WM20 II, WM18 II

Population	10,414,336

2 filets pikeperch

2 lbs. white asparagus (peeled)

1 potato

½ onion

1 small leek (white part)

1 knob butter

4 pt. fish stock

1 cube vegetable broth (bouillon)

1 c. double cream

Garnish

Chervil

Finely chop the vegetables. (It is important to finely cut the asparagus to avoid fibres when cooked.) Put the asparagus tips aside. They will be added to the soup at the end.

Melt the butter and add the vegetables. Cook them for about 6 minutes with the lid on (steaming the asparagus in this way intensifies the flavour). Avoid cooking them too long, as discolouring may occur and it might taste burned. Add the fish stock together with the vegetable broth. Boil for 35 minutes. Blend the soup, preferably in a blender to ensure smooth consistency so that it is free of fibres.

Add salt and pepper to taste. Add the cream. Add the asparagus tips either pre-steamed or raw if crispy texture is preferred. Season the pike with salt and pepper and fry in butter on the skin (the skin should be crispy). Place the pike filets on the soup and garnish with chervil.

ASPARAGUS SOUP
WITH PIKEPERCH

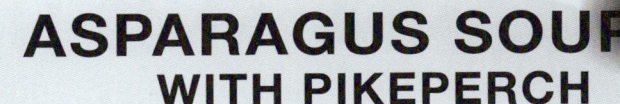

BOSNIA AND HERZEGOVINA

BOSNIA AND HERZEGOVINA'S HOCKEY HISTORY

Bosnia and Herzegovina became the 61st member of the IIHF during the 2001 Annual Congress. The country made its debut at the World Championships in 2004, when its junior U18 team played in Division III. Currently, there is no organized national hockey championship in Bosnia and Herzegovina.

ICE HOCKEY IN BOSNIA AND HERZEGOVINA

Federation	
Registered Players:	249
Senior:	75
Juvenile:	168
Female:	6
Referees	
Male:	5
Female:	0
Rinks	
Indoor:	2
Outdoor:	1
Participation	-
Population	4,613,414

1 lb. chicken pieces (with bones)

½ lb. carrots, parsley,
and 1 celery root (peeled)

1 tbsp. butter

1 tbsp. plain flour

1 oz. okra (whole, stalk removed)

1 egg yolk

2 oz. sour cream

Juice of 1 lemon

1 bay leaf

1 tbsp. salt and pepper

If using dried okra, soak well in water. Rinse thoroughly.

Cook the okra in slightly salted water (water just covering the vegetables). Add half of the lemon juice. Once the okra is cooked, drain and set aside. Rinse the chicken pieces, and place in a stock pot with water and salt. Add carrots, parsley, celery, and the bay leaf. Simmer until the chicken is cooked. Sieve the soup setting the broth aside to cool.

Remove the bones from the chicken and dice the meat as well as the vegetables. Set aside. Melt the butter in a deep pan, add flour and parch it. Add the cooled broth stirring continuously and simmer for about 15 minutes. Add meat and vegetables to broth and simmer. When the vegetables are cooked add the okra and simmer. Take it off the heat. Beat the egg yolk with the sour cream, and add it to the soup. Add lemon juice, butter, and pepper to taste.

BEY'S SOUP

BRAZIL

BRAZIL'S HOCKEY HISTORY

The first official games in Brazil were played in 1967 in the ice hall of the Hotel Quitandinha. Games took place there for eight years until the hotel was closed. Hockey resumed in 1978 with teams playing on a rink used for Holiday on Ice. It was Dietenhofer whose efforts made possible the creation of the Confederacao Brasileira de Desportos Terrestres (Brazil Ice Sport Union) and the organization Brazil Hockey as part of the sports union. He served as the first president of both Brazil Hockey and the Brazil Ice Sport Union. Brazil joined the IIHF in November 1984.

ICE HOCKEY IN BRAZIL

Federation

Registered Players:	n/a
Senior:	n/a
Juvenile:	n/a
Female:	n/a

Referees

Male:	n/a
Female:	n/a

Rinks

Indoor:	n/a
Outdoor:	n/a
Participation	-
Population	198,739,269

2 tbsp. cooking oil

1 onion (chopped)

1 green bell pepper (chopped)

3 cloves garlic (minced)

¾ c. rice (long-grain)

¼ tsp. red pepper (crushed)

1¾ tsp. salt

11 oz. tomatoes (finely cubed)

1 tbsp. tomato paste

2 pt. water

1 c. coconut milk (canned, unsweetened)

8 medium-sized shrimps
(hulled, cut horizontally in ½)

¼ tsp. black pepper (fresh ground)

1 tbsp. lemon juice

½ c. fresh parsley or cilantro
(finely chopped)

Garnish
4 cooked shrimps (with tails)

In a large pot, heat the oil over moderately low heat. Add the onion, bell pepper, and garlic and cook, stirring occasionally, until the vegetables start to soften, about 10 minutes.

Add the rice, red pepper flakes, salt, tomatoes, and water to the pot. Bring to a boil and cook until the rice is almost tender, about 10 minutes.

Stir the coconut milk into the soup. Bring back to a simmer and then stir in the shrimps. Simmer, stirring occasionally, until the shrimps are just done, 3-5 minutes. Stir in the black pepper, lemon juice, and parsley. Before serving, garnish with whole shrimps.

BRAZILIAN SOUP

BULGARIA

BULGARIA'S HOCKEY HISTORY

Hockey in Bulgaria began in 1929 when the Bulgarian Skating Club was created. Hockey became increasingly popular in Bulgaria and in 1950, five new sports clubs were founded, each with their own hockey team. In 1952, the country's first national championship took place. Bulgaria's first artificial ice rink opened in Sofia in 1960. After joining the IIHF on July 25, 1963, Bulgaria began to play at the World Championship. It debuted at the 1963 «C» Pool Championship and remained chiefly at that level until 1991 after which it played mostly on Division II or Division III level.

ICE HOCKEY IN BULGARIA

Federation

Registered Players:	303
Senior:	114
Juvenile:	189
Female:	27

Referees

Male:	30
Female:	3

Rinks

Indoor:	3
Outdoor:	5

Participation
WM II, WM20 III, WM18 III

Population	7,204,687

BULGARIA
ICE HOCKEY
FEDERATION

1 large cucumber
(peeled, seeded, chopped)

4 cloves garlic

½ tsp. salt

¼ c. walnuts

2 slices day-old white sandwich bread
(without crust, torn into pieces)

2 tbsp. sunflower, walnut or olive oil

1½ c. yogurt

1-2 tsp. lemon juice

½ cup cold water

Garnish

½ cup walnuts (coarsely chopped)

1½ tbsp. olive oil

Fresh dill

Using a food processor, pureé garlic, salt, ¼ cup walnuts and bread. Slowly add oil through food shoot and process until well combined. Transfer mixture to a large bowl and beat in the yogurt, cucumber and lemon juice. At this point, the mixture can be served as a dip. Otherwise, for soup, add water and leave chunky or puree until smooth.

Refrigerate until ready to serve. Pour soup into chilled bowls and garnish with ½ cup coarsely chopped walnuts, a few drops of oil and fresh dill.

COLD CUCUMBER SOUP

ICE HOCKEY IN CANADA

Federation

Registered Players:	499695
Senior:	88954
Juvenile:	325432
Female:	85309

Referees

Male:	29839
Female:	1365

Rinks

Indoor:	2451
Outdoor:	11000

Participation

WM, WW, WM20, WM18, WW18

Population   33,487,208

CANADA

CANADA'S HOCKEY HISTORY

The game of hockey was born in Canada. And still today, Canada is the largest country that plays the sport. Hockey is played in every part of the country, which boasts both amateur and professional leagues and clubs. Internationally, Canada is also dominant, thanks in large part of the creation of Hockey Canada in 1969. Beginning with 1972's famed eight-game series with the Soviet Union, professional players began participating in some international events. Canada dominated play during the history of the Canada Cup tournament (1976 to 1991), an event which let Team Canada employ its very best professional stars. Canada has enjoyed an excellent period since 2002, with dominating performances in men's, women's and U20 juniors.

4 c. vegetable bouillon

1 meaty ham bone (loin chop)

2 slices bacon (including the rind)

½ lb. dry split peas

1 onion (chopped)

2 carrots (grated)

1 bay leaf

1 tsp. prepared mustard

Plenty of ground pepper

Salt

Dice the bacon slices in small cubes. Fry the onions and bacon. Add the stock, the meat, the peas, the carrots, the bacon rind and the spices. Cook for 45 minutes, or until the peas are tender. Remove the bacon rind and discard. Take out the meat and slice before arranging on the soup.

PEA SOUP

CHINA'S HOCKEY HISTORY

The roots of Chinese ice hockey date back to 1915 when a few games took place in Sen Jan Province. The Ice Hockey Association of the People's Republic of China was founded in 1951. The first national championship was held in 1953. In 1956, the Chinese national team made its debut. China joined the IIHF on July 25, 1963. It played its first game in the «C» Pool World Championship in 1972 and since that time has played on either Division I or Division II levels. Domestic hockey has been centred in the northern provinces.

CHINA

ICE HOCKEY IN CHINA

Federation

Registered Players:	448
Senior:	101
Juvenile:	181
Female:	166

Referees

Male:	34
Female:	11

Rinks

Indoor:	40
Outdoor:	36

Participation

WM II, WW, WM20 III, WM18 II

Population 1,338,612,968

Olive oil for frying

½ lb. rice noodles

2 pt. beef stock

½ lb. soy sprouts

½ c. of young spinach

1 bn. mint (finely chopped)

1 tbsp. sugar

For the marinade and meat

2 tsp. light soy sauce

1 tbsp. peanut butter (salted)

1 tsp. Sambal Oelek

1 tbsp. coconut (grated)

1 tbsp. sugar

12 oz. boiling beef (cut in fine slices)
For the marinade mix all ingredients.
Rub the marinade into the beef, cover and
refrigerate for 2 hours.

Put noodles in a pan, pour boiling salted water over them and let soak for 10 minutes. Drain well and cut into 6 inch long strips. Set aside. In a large frying pan (or wok) heat the oil and fry the marinated meat in small portions until crispy. Place the crispy beef into the individual soup bowls.

Using the same frying pan bring the stock to a boil. Add the soy sprouts, spinach, chopped mint and the sugar. Bring to a boil. Add the noodles and serve over the meat. Just before serving, garnish with peanuts and mint leaves.

Garnish
2 tbsp. peanuts (salted, roughly chopped)
A few chopped mint leaves
4 pre-warmed soup bowls

SPICY BEEF NOODLE SOUP

CHINESE TAIPEI

CHINESE TAIPEI'S HOCKEY HISTORY

The Chinese Taipei Skating Association was founded in 1980. Two years later the first national championship took place. In 1983, Chinese Taipei became a member of the IIHF. The debut of the Chinese Taipei national team was in 1987 at the «D» Pool World Championship. The national team tied Hong Kong, 2–2, in its first official game on March 13, 1987.

ICE HOCKEY IN CHINESE TAIPEI

Federation

Registered Players:	851
Senior:	307
Juvenile:	456
Female:	88

Referees

Male:	81
Female:	8

Rinks

Indoor:	1
Outdoor:	10

Participation

WM18 III

Population	21,003,976

6 oz. lean pork

½ tbsp. soy sauce

1 tbsp. cornstarch paste

10 oz. fish paste

4 black mushrooms

1 cup bok choy
(Chinese cabbage, shredded)

½ c. carrot (shredded)

6 c. boiling water

1 tbsp. soy sauce

1 tsp. salt

3 tbsp. cornstarch paste

Make a paste from pressed garlic, parsley, pepper, sesame oil, vinegar (little of each).

Slice the pork into small, long pieces. Soak in soy sauce and cornstarch paste for around 20 minutes. Then mix with fish paste.

Boil 6 cups of water and then add shredded bok choy, carrots and the black mushrooms. Cook it for 15 minutes until the cabbage is soft. Then start to add the pork mixture into the soup piece by piece and cook with low heat for 3 minutes. Season with soy sauce, salt and thicken with cornstarch paste. Before serving the soup, season with the herb paste. Serve hot.

MEAT POTAGE

CROATIA'S HOCKEY HISTORY

In 1991, the Croatian Ice Hockey Association was founded and the first Croatian national championship was won by MK Zagreb in 1991–92. The nation joined the IIHF on May 6, 1992, and the Croatian national team made its debut in the 1994 «C» Pool World Championship. Croatia is currently in a process of establishing themselves on the Division I level.

ICE HOCKEY IN CROATIA

Federation

Registered Players:	591
Senior:	113
Juvenile:	436
Female:	42

Referees

Male:	10
Female:	1

Rinks

Indoor:	2
Outdoor:	4

Participation

WM I, WM20 II, WM18 II

Population	4,489,409

CROATIA

2 tbsp. olive oil

3 red onions (finely chopped)

4 oz. smoked bacon (finely chopped)

1 lb. button mushrooms (finely chopped)

2 tbsp. plain flour

3 c. vegetable stock

1 sweet red pepper (finely chopped)

3 waxy potatoes (diced)

¼ c. white wine

1 tbsp. prepared mustard

1 tsp. chili powder

1 bay leaf

Pepper

Vegetable salt

Garnish

Parsley

Fry the onions in the olive oil. When glazed, add the chopped bacon followed by the mushrooms. Add the flour and the red pepper. Add the stock as well as the other spices and the wine. In the meantime, cook the diced potatoes in salted water. Thereafter add the potatoes to the soup and cook for 10 minutes before serving. Add more spices if necessary. Garnish with parsley.

ZAGORSKA SOUP

THE CZECH REPUBLIC'S HOCKEY HISTORY

The game of ice hockey was demonstrated for the first time at Prague in 1905 by Canada's Ruck Anderson. In 1911, the Bohemian National Team won the European Championship. The Czechoslovakian National Team won European titles again in 1922, 1925, 1929, and 1933. After the fall of Communism, the Czech Republic and Slovakia replaced Czechoslovakia in the IIHF. The Czech Republic's first major triumph took place at the 1996 World Championship when the team won gold on a last-minute goal versus Canada. The high point in Czech hockey circles was the stunning gold medal victory at the 1998 Nagano Olympics. This started a formidable period during which the Czechs won gold at the World Championships in 1999, 2000, 2001 and 2005.

ICE HOCKEY IN THE CZECH REPUBLIC

Federation

Registered Players:	97102
Senior:	62487
Juvenile:	32623
Female:	1992

Referees

Male:	3474
Female:	46

Rinks

Indoor:	157
Outdoor:	23

Participation

WM, WW I, WM20, WM18, WW18

Population 10,211,904

CZECH REPUBLIC

1 lb. tripe

5 oz. ham (cut in strips)

1 carrot (cut into small slices)

¼ celery root (cut into small slices)

1 garlic clove (pressed)

4 tbsp. flour

1 pn. pepper

1 pn. marjoram

1 tbsp. ginger (freshly ground)

2 tbsp. butter

Parsley

Salt

Wash the tripe well in cold water, cook for ½ hour, drain and rinse well in cold water. Cut the tripe in small slices and set aside. Put 2 pints of water in a pan; add salt, carrot, parsley and celery. Cook until tender. Remove two ladles of liquid and set aside to cool. In a separate pan heat the butter; add the flour and heat until golden brown (stirring continuously). Pour the cooled liquid into the browned flour and stir, making sure no lumps of flour remain. Add mixture to the remainder of the soup and season with the garlic, pepper, marjoram, chopped parsley and ginger. Cook well. Add tripe and meat. Serve when tripe and ham are warm.

CZECH TRIPE SOUP

DENMARK

DENMARK'S HOCKEY HISTORY

Informal games were played in Copenhagen as early as the 1920s. The popularization of the game was enhanced by the creation of the Denmarks Ishockey Union in 1949. Denmark became a member of the IIHF on April 27, 1946. After a tough debut in 1949, the national team did not return to the World Championship until the 1962 «B» Pool tournament. Between 1963–1991, the Danes competed for the most part in «C» Pool. The Danes remained a fixture at the «B» Pool level throughout the 1990s, but are today considered as maybe the most improved program in men's ice hockey, permanently among the Top 16.

ICE HOCKEY IN DENMARK

Federation

Registered Players:	4059
Senior:	1719
Juvenile:	2038
Female:	301

Referees

Male:	74
Female:	3

Rinks

Indoor:	22
Outdoor:	0

Participation
WM, WW II, WM20 I, WM18 I

Population	5,500,510

8 scallops

Tomatoes (peeled, finely chopped)

Celery stalks (finely shredded)

Oil

Basil (finely chopped)

Coriander

Salt and pepper

For the stock

3 lbs. ripe tomatoes

1 tsp. salt

1 tsp. sugar

Slice the tomatoes. Mix the sugar and salt, and season the tomatoes with the mixture. Place them in a fine sieve over a stock pan. Leave to drain overnight. On the next day remove the sieve and add 1 litre of water to the tomato juice and bring to a boil.

Lightly scar the scallops on the surface, brush with the oil and season with salt, pepper and coriander. Grill only on one side, so they remain firm for cutting. Heat up the tomato stock and serve in warmed bowl. In the middle of each bowl, place a small pile of tomato, celery and basil and arrange the grilled scallops around it.

CLEAR TOMATO BOUILLON
WITH GRILLED SCALLOPS

DPR KOREA'S HOCKEY HISTORY

Ice hockey in the Democratic People's Republic of Korea became popular in the 50s when Soviet and Chinese workers taught the game in Pyongyang. The Ice Hockey Association of the Democratic People's Republic of Korea was founded in 1955. North Korea became a member of the IIHF on August 8, 1964. The national team made its debut in 1974 in the «C» Pool World Championship. The first national championship was held in 1956, and was won by Amnokang Pyongyang. The women's team made its international debut in 2000. Since 2001, the team has played in Division I.

ICE HOCKEY ASSOCIATION
DPR KOREA

DPR KOREA

ICE HOCKEY IN DPR KOREA

Federation

Registered Players:	3270
Senior:	480
Juvenile:	1940
Female:	850

Referees

Male:	35
Female:	15

Rinks

Indoor:	3
Outdoor:	15

Participation

WM II, WW II, WM20 III

Population   22,665,345

3 lbs. gray mullet

1 tsp. salt

1 tsp. fresh ginger (grated)

1 tsp. garlic (pressed)

1 pn. black pepper

Garnish
2 spring onions (finely chopped)

Cut the gray mullet in small pieces. Pour cold water into pot, wrap black pepper in white cloth (form a small bag), boil the gray mullet together with the black pepper. Add salt according to taste. Grind ginger and garlic. When the gray mullet is ready, serve it in a saucer and add ginger and garlic to the soup. Garnish with spring onions.

GRAY MULLET SOUP
FROM RIVER TAEDONG

ESTONIA'S HOCKEY HISTORY

The Estonian Ice Hockey Federation was founded in 1921 when Estonia was an independent country and was re-founded in 1991 as a part of the Soviet Ice Hockey Federation. The first national championship was in 1934 and won by Kalev Tallinn. Estonia originally joined the IIHF in 1937. The national team played its first game on February 20, 1937, losing 2–1 to Finland. The newly independent nation of Estonia became a member of the IIHF on May 6, 1992 and has since then been a solid Division I nation.

ESTONIA

ICE HOCKEY IN ESTONIA

Federation

Registered Players:	950
Senior:	353
Juvenile:	512
Female:	85

Referees

Male:	142
Female:	12

Rinks

Indoor:	8
Outdoor:	5

Participation

WM II, WM20 I, WM18 II

Population 1,299,371

3 lbs. knuckle of pork

1 lb. dried green split peas (rinsed, drained)

1 large onion (diced)

1 celery stalk (diced)

1 large carrot (peeled, diced)

2 pt. vegetable stock

6-8 parsley stalks

1 bay leaf

½ tsp. black pepper (freshly ground)

½ tsp. salt (optional)

Garnish

Croutons

Put the knuckle of pork into a large stockpot together with the vegetable stock and bring gently to a boil. Add the peas, onion, celery, and carrots. Tie the parsley springs and bay leaf into a cheesecloth bundle and add it to the soup. Turn the heat to high and bring the soup to a boil again. Cover, lower the heat to a simmer, and cook for 1½-2 hours. Remove the knuckle of as well as the cheesecloth bundle. Remove the meat from the bone and set the meat aside. Let the soup cool slightly and then blend it in batches. Meanwhile, dice the meat into ½-inch cubes. Add 3 or 4 cups of the ham back into the blended soup. Simmer and season with pepper. Add salt if necessary. Serve with croutons on top and mustard.

SPLIT PEA SOUP
WITH HAM

ICE HOCKEY IN FINLAND

Federation

Registered Players:	61684
Senior:	21746
Juvenile:	36411
Female:	3527

Referees

Male:	1607
Female:	37

Rinks

Indoor:	220
Outdoor:	27

Participation

WM, WW, WM20, WM18, WW18

Population	5,250,275

FINLAND

FINLAND'S HOCKEY HISTORY

The first club game was played in Tampere on January 15, 1928. Finland was admitted to the IIHF on February 10, 1928. The first artificial rink in Finland did not open until November 22, 1955 in Tampere. Finland's national team was a force in the 60s. By the 80s players such as Jari Kurri, Esa Tikkanen and Reijo Routsalainen were NHL stars. The 1988 Calgary Olympics saw the Finns shock the USSR 2–1 to earn the silver medal, and four years later they finished second to Sweden at the World Championship. Finland won the bronze medal at the 1994 Olympics and reached an all time high winning the 1995 world Championship gold. It was one of many medals the Finns claimed in the next decade.

14 oz. salmon (cubes of 3cm)

14 oz. potatoes (diced)

2 carrots (diced)

1-2 onions

3½ c. fish stock

1 c. cream (milk)

1 bay leaf

1 tbsp. butter

1 bn. dill (chopped)

Salt and pepper

Garnish

Rye bread

Finely chop the onions and fry gently in a large stock pan. Add the carrots and potatoes. Fry shortly before adding the fish stock and bay leaf. Cook until the potatoes are tender. Add the salmon and cream and season to taste. Turn the heat off and leave for 3-4 minutes prior to serving. Garnish with dill and serve with rye bread.

SALMON SOUP

FRANCE

FRANCE'S HOCKEY HISTORY

France held its first national hockey championship in 1904. The national team played its first game against Belgium in 1906. Two years later, France, England, Belgium, and Switzerland founded the eventual IIHF. On October 20, 1908, France became the first member of the new organization and Frenchman Louis Magnus became its first president. The French alternated between «B» and «C» Pools in the 1960s before settling into the latter between 1970 and 1985. France won the 1985 «C» Pool competition to earn promotion to «B» Pool where they played for five years. The national team is currently ranked 14th in the world, and trying to become a solid Top-16 nation.

ICE HOCKEY IN FRANCE

Federation

Registered Players:	17133
Senior:	6041
Juvenile:	9572
Female:	1520

Referees

Male:	120
Female:	10

Rinks

Indoor:	130
Outdoor:	24

Participation

WM, WW I, WM20 I, WM18 I, WW18 I

Population   64,057,792

For the stock

2-3 whole fish bones from the flat fish

1 oz. butter

1 bay leaf

6-8 fennel seeds (crushed)

3 oz. button mushrooms

2 oz. leek

2 oz. root celery

2 shallot onions

Dill

½ c. white wine

1¼ c. water

Rinse the fish bones well and chop into small pieces. Chop the vegetables into small pieces and sauté in the butter. Add the fish bones and quench with the white wine. Add the water and bring to a boil. Reduce the heat and simmer for 1 hour. Sieve off the stock and set it aside.

For the soup

Small leek

½ fennel

1 onion (chopped)

1 celery stalk

2 tomatoes

1 small carrot

Saffron

Olive oil

Salt and pepper

Chop the vegetables finely. Sauté gently with the saffron in the olive oil. Lay the fish over the vegetables and poor the hot stock over it. Important: Do not cook any further, but just let it stand (2-3 minutes).

Sauce Rouille

1 small chili

4 cloves garlic

½ red pepper

6 slices white toast (without the crust)

½ c. olive oil

1 egg yolk

1 bn. basil

Place all the ingredients in a cutter and blend thoroughly.

Select fresh fish from the market, eg. trout, salmon, crawfish, pikeperch (with skin), catfish. Alternatively seafood, eg. sole, red mullet, monkfish, tiger prawns. Whole fish: 3 lbs. of which 1 lb. filets. Filet the fish and portion it, cook a stock with the fish leftovers.

BOUILLABAISSE
WITH SAUCE ROUILLE

GERMANY'S HOCKEY HISTORY

The beginning of ice sports in Germany goes back to 1888 when the country's National Skating Union was founded in Berlin. On September 19, 1909, Germany became the sixth nation to join the IIHF. Germany quickly became among the best in Europe and never failed to win a medal at the European Championships through 1914. The West German national team played in the 1984 Canada Cup. Their roster included Erich Kuhnhackl, the best known West German player up to this point. Another prominent name was that of Udo Kiessling who was selected to the World Championship All-Star Team in 1987. Germany has taken part in the 2002 and 2006 Olympics and they also qualified for Vancouver 2010.

ICE HOCKEY IN GERMANY

Federation

Registered Players:	28967
Senior:	8656
Juvenile:	17817
Female:	2494

Referees

Male:	799
Female:	66

Rinks

Indoor:	175
Outdoor:	44

Participation

WM, WW I, WM20, WM18, WW18

Population 82,329,758

GERMANY

2 lbs. beef bones with meat

2 carrots

1 celery root

1 leek

1 clove garlic

7 oz. minced meat (pork)

3½ oz. minced meat (beef)

5 oz. veal liver (roughly chopped, chop by hand to avoid it becoming liquid)

3 dry rolls (diced, soaked in milk)

1 large onion

2 eggs

Nutmeg

Marjoram

Oil

Salt and pepper

1 bn. parsley

1 bn. chives

Stock

Put beef bones into a stock pot and fill with 2½ quarts of water. Cut vegetables into big chunks and add to soup. Season with salt, pepper and nutmeg. Cook the stock for 1½ hours. Strain soup and set the stock aside.

Dumplings

Place the mincemeat and chopped liver in a bowl. Squeeze all the milk out of the buns and add the bread to the meat. Finely chop chives and parsley. Dice onions in sauté in butter until glazed. Add 1 tsp. of marjoram to the onions and stir and add to the meat. Season with salt and pepper. Add the eggs, the bread as well as the parsley and chives (put a handful aside for garnish). Mix everything gently but thoroughly by hand.

Bring stock to a quick boil. Form dumplings by hand and place them carefully into the simmering stock. Let dumplings simmer for approximately 30 minutes. Garnish with some chives prior to serving.

BAVARIAN LIVER DUMPLING SOUP

ICE HOCKEY IN GREAT BRITAIN

Federation

Registered Players:	5627
Senior:	1191
Juvenile:	3853
Female:	583

Referees

Male:	260
Female:	17

Rinks

Indoor:	44
Outdoor:	0

Participation

WM I, WW II, WM20 II, WM18 II

Population	61,113,205

GREAT BRITAIN

GREAT BRITAIN'S HOCKEY HISTORY

Skates with metal blades were introduced to Britain from Holland around 1600 and in 1642 the Edinburgh Skating Club was formed. Many sketches and paintings during the 18th and 19th century depict people skating on frozen lakes and rivers, often using sticks and a ball. The first official ice hockey game played outside of Canada is said to have been Cambridge University versus Oxford University at St. Moritz, Switzerland in 1885. The first English Ice Hockey League was formed in 1903 with the London Canadians winning the first title. In 1908, England joined France, Belgium, and Switzerland in founding the IIHF. Britain remained a hockey power in Europe until World War II. The culmination of their success took place at the 1936 Garmisch-Partenkirchen Olympics when they stunned Canada 2–1 to win the gold medal. The had a short stint on top level (1994), but are usually to be found in Division I.

57

8 oz. shin of beef

2 lbs. beef bones
(marrow bones if possible)

2 carrots (finely chopped)

2 onions (finely chopped)

2 leeks (finely chopped)

2 celery sticks (finely chopped)

1 egg white
(beaten to a dropping consistency)

Salt and pepper (freshly ground)

1 glass sherry

Garnish

Cheese straws

Put the meat, bones and vegetables with a good pinch of salt into a large pan and cover with nearly 5 pints of cold water. Add the beaten egg white last. Bring slowly to a boil, whisking energetically from time to time, until the white of the egg and impurities form a frothy lid on the top. Allow to simmer for 2½ hours. Rinse a tea towel in cold water, place it in a colander and then strain the broth through the cloth into the bowl. Repeat the process until last traces of egg white foam are removed from the soup. Season to taste.

At this stage, if the potage is to be served hot, return it to a clean pan. If it is to be served cold let it cool and put it into the refrigerator. It must be either piping hot or properly chilled. The sherry, like all fortified wines, has a short-lived flavour and should be added almost at the last moment, just before serving. Serve with cheese straws.

ENGLISH POTAGE

GREECE

GREECE'S HOCKEY HISTORY

Ice hockey in Greece was introduced by Czechoslovak emigrants in the early 1980s. Ice was only available for about two or three weeks in November. Greece joined the IIHF in April of 1987. The first Greek national hockey championship took place in 1988–89. In 1989, Greece's ice hockey association became a section of the Greek Ice Sports Federation. Three years later, the Greek National Team made its international debut at the «C» Pool World Championship where they defeated Turkey, 15–3 on March 21, 1992. They also vanquished Israel and Luxembourg to win the bronze medal. Greece is currently on the Division III level.

ICE HOCKEY IN GREECE

Federation

Registered Players:	596
Senior:	457
Juvenile:	76
Female:	63

Referees

Male:	5
Female:	0

Rinks

Indoor:	1
Outdoor:	2

Participation
WM III

Population	10,737,428

1 lb. mixed mincemeat (veal/pork)

1 onion (finely chopped)

1 carrot (in rings)

1 sprig celery (sliced)

3 level tbsp. rice for the soup

5 c. water

Juice of 2 lemons

2 eggs

3 tbsp olive oil

Salt and pepper

Garnish

Marjoram

Mix the mincemeat with the onions, salt, pepper, rice and add some olive oil. Then form the mixture into small balls the size of a walnut.

Put 5 cups of water into a pan and bring it to a boil. Add the meatballs, the carrots, the celery and three spoonfuls of olive oil. Let it simmer for about 1 hour. Separate the eggs and beat the egg white until stiff. In a separate bowl mix the egg yolk with the lemon juice until creamy. Add the stiff egg white and mix gently. Now add a few spoons of the hot broth very slowly to the mixture. Stir constantly to avoid the eggs separating. Pour the mixture gently back into the soup. Garnish with marjoram leaves.

MEATBALL SOUP
WITH RICE

ICE HOCKEY IN HUNGARY

Federation

Registered Players:	2034
Senior:	329
Juvenile:	1594
Female:	111

Referees

Male:	56
Female:	6

Rinks

Indoor:	17
Outdoor:	11

Participation
WM, WM20 I, WM18 I

Population	9,905,596

HUNGARY

HUNGARY'S HOCKEY HISTORY

The Hungarian Winter Sports Federation was founded in 1908. Hungary joined the IIHF on January 24, 1927, and that same day the Hungarian National Team played its first game, losing 6–0 to Austria. Hungary's first artificial ice rink was built outdoors at Budapest in 1926. The Hungarians managed a 1–1 tie against gold-medal-winning Canadian team at the 1938 World Championship. World War II stopped the development of hockey in Hungary for nearly 10 years, but interest in the game rose again by the late 1940s. In subsequent years, training methods were significantly improved by Czechoslovakian coach Vladimir Kominek, who led the Hungarian National Team between 1959 and 1964. Most recently, Hungary earned a promotion to the top level world championship in 2009—its first appearance among the elite nations in 70 years.

12 oz. beef (without bones, finely cubed)

3 oz. lard

1 onion (chopped)

½ oz. paprika

1½ lbs. firm cooking potatoes (finely cubed)

6 oz. bell peppers (finely cubed)

2 oz. tomatoes (finely cubed)

2 pt. beef stock

Garlic

Caraway

Salt

Garnish

Chives (finely cut)

Lemon peel (finely graded)

Melt the lard in a pan and fry the onions until they are golden. Lower the heat, mix in the paprika and add the beef. Salt lightly and continue to fry. Once the meat juice has evaporated, add the garlic and caraway. Add some of the beef stock, cover and stew, stirring occasionally. Continue to add small portions of the beef stock and stew until meat is tender (only add stock if the liquid is completely reduced).

Add the potatoes, bell peppers and tomatoes and fry with the meat until tender. Add the rest of the beef stock and simmer for 15 minutes. Season to taste.

GOULASH SOUP

ICELAND

ICELAND'S HOCKEY HISTORY

Hockey in Iceland dates back to 1937. The main hockey playing centre was the North Sea port of Akureyri followed by the capital, Reykjavik. The Icelandic Skating Association was created in 1987. Iceland joined the IIHF on May 6, 1992, and made its debut on the world stage in 1997 when its National Junior team played at the «D» Pool European Junior Championship. The country recorded its first win at an IIHF tournament, defeating Turkey 4–2. In 1999, they debuted in the World Senior Championship in the «D» Pool, and are currently a Division II nation.

ICE HOCKEY IN ICELAND

Federation

Registered Players:	599
Senior:	64
Juvenile:	467
Female:	68

Referees

Male:	22
Female:	3

Rinks

Indoor:	3
Outdoor:	0

Participation
WM II, WM20 III, WM18 III

Population	306,694

3 lbs. lamb shoulder on the bone

1 onion (sliced)

3 pt. meat stock

2 tbsp. dried herbs and mixed vegetables

1 lb. rutabaga (½-inch dices)

4 potatoes (peeled, ½-inch dices)

4 carrots (peeled, ¼-inch dices)

1 tsp. salt

Black pepper (freshly ground)

Traditionally, fatty meat is used, but now many prefer to remove most of the fat. Place the meat and onion in a large pan and pour cold water over it. Bring to a boil. Let the soup boil rapidly for a few minutes and then skim it. Add dried vegetables and some salt and pepper and simmer for around 40 minutes. Add rutabagas, potatoes and carrots and cook gently for 20-25 more minutes, or until all the vegetables are tender. Season to taste.

The meat is either cut into small cubes and returned to the soup or removed, cut and served on a separate platter. In any case it is always eaten with the soup.

TRADITIONAL ICELANDIC MEAT SOUP

ICE HOCKEY IN INDIA

Federation

Registered Players:	n/a
Senior:	n/a
Juvenile:	n/a
Female:	n/a
Referees	
Male:	n/a
Female:	n/a
Rinks	
Indoor:	n/a
Outdoor:	n/a
Participation	-
Population	1,166,079,217

INDIA

INDIA'S HOCKEY HISTORY

Ice hockey is fairly new in India, but it is played passionately in the Himalayan areas of Ladakh and Himachal which have natural ice surfaces during the winter months. In the early 80s, soldiers and the local youth started playing the game to occupy themselves throughout the long winter. They used improvised field hockey sticks and used shoe polish tins as pucks. Even though no artificial rinks have yet to be built in India, the game flourishes during the winters.

The Ice Hockey Association of India (IHAI) organizes competitions and training programs to develop players and give them exposure to international competition. Together with IHAI, coaches and players from Canada and the United States living in India have greatly helped Indian teams to gather equipment and promote the game. To date, more than 25 hockey clubs are operating in India of which seven play at the national level. In March 2009, IHAI sent its first ever national ice hockey team to Abu Dhabi for an international tournament, the Asian Challenge Cup.

½ lb. lamb

1 lb. lamb bones

½ lb. onions (sliced)

1 tbsp. ginger-garlic paste

1 tsp. chili powder

1 tsp. turmeric

4 c. coconut milk

Juice of 2 lemons

Oil

For the masala

1¼ tbsp. coriander seeds

1¼ tbsp. peanuts

1¼ tbsp. poppy seeds

1½ tbsp. chironji (melon seeds)

1 tbsp. cumin

2 tbsp. gram (chickpeas)

Lightly roast the ingredients and grind thereafter.

Boil lamb and bones with 4 cups water for about 1-1½ hours and set aside the stock. Cut cooked lamb into small pieces.

Fry onions in a little oil. Add ginger-garlic paste, chili powder, turmeric and salt and fry well. Now add all the ground masala and fry until cooked. Add the stock to the masala and cook. When ready, strain through a muslin cloth. Add coconut milk and cook for a few minutes. Finally, add lamb pieces and lemon juice. Serve hot.

MULLIGATAWNY SOUP

IRELAND

IRELAND'S HOCKEY HISTORY

Ice hockey in Ireland did not gain popularity until the 1980s when the game's supporters formed new teams. Much of the activity took place in Dublin. The first official game took place on April 21, 1982. Ireland made its IIHF debut at the European Junior Championship Division II. In 2001, the Dublin City Council recruited the IIHA to help out in running an outdoor rink in the centre of Dublin. Once again the players both junior and senior had home ice. The rink is open every year and provides a training ground for all the IIHA members and up-and-coming stars. The IIHA submitted its first senior men's national squad to IIHF competition in 2004. Ireland was back on the map.

ICE HOCKEY IN IRELAND

Federation

Registered Players:	499
Senior:	277
Juvenile:	185
Female:	37

Referees

Male:	37
Female:	44

Rinks

Indoor:	4
Outdoor:	2

Participation
WM III, WM18 III

Population	4,203,200

2 oz. Kerrygold butter

3 medium-sized brown onions (peeled, diced)

2 leeks (thinly sliced)

5 potatoes (1½-cm cubes)

⅓ c. barley

2 c. chicken stock

2 c. full-fat milk

Nutmeg (ground)

Pepper (ground)

Garnish

Chives (chopped)

Parsley

Croutons

Whipped cream

Melt the butter gently in a large heavy based pan and cook the onions and leeks for 3 minutes. Add the potatoes and continue to cook until the potatoes are golden brown. Separately boil the barley in water, drain and leave to cool. Add the barley to the potatoes. Reduce the heat and stir in the stock and milk.

Simmer for 30 minutes or until the vegetables are tender and the soup has been thickened by the potatoes. Season to taste with salt, pepper and nutmeg. Garnish with chives, parsley and croutons (roasted in bacon fat). Alternatively garnish with whipped cream.

POTATO AND LEEK SOUP

ISRAEL

ISRAEL'S HOCKEY HISTORY

Israel's first rink opened in January 1986, in northern Israel. Practices began in April with former Canadian players as instructors. In May, 1988, a larger rink opened near Tel Aviv. That same year, the Israel Ice Hockey Association was founded. Israel joined the IIHF on May 2, 1991. The national team made its debut at the «C» Pool World Championship in 1992, losing its first game 23–4 against Spain. A few days later, Israel recorded its first win, defeating Turkey, 8–2. Israeli hockey has received a major boost in 1995 with the opening of an almost Olympic-sized skating rink at the Canada Centre in Metulla.

ICE HOCKEY IN ISRAEL
Federation
Registered Players:	500
Senior:	120
Juvenile:	380
Female:	28

Referees
Male:	4
Female:	0

Rinks
Indoor:	1
Outdoor:	0

Participation
WM II, WM18 III

Population	7,233,701

1 qt. water

1 large chicken
(preferably stewing or large roaster)

2 whole onions (cut in ½)

2 parsnips (peeled, left whole)

2 stalks celery and their leaves
(finely chopped)

1 kohlrabi (½ of it cubed)

3 carrots
(peeled, 2 left whole, 1 finely cut)

1 zucchini (finely cubed)

2 bn. parsley (finely chopped)

1 bn. dill (snipped)

1 tbsp. salt

½ tsp. pepper

Garnish
4 small sprigs dill

Cut out the back bone of the chicken, put it in a pan and bring to a boil. Skim off the froth. Add the onions, 1 parsnip, the celery, ½ kohlrabi, 2 carrots, ½ of the parsley, salt and pepper. Cover and simmer for 30 minutes, season to taste.

Strain the soup into a clean pan, remove the chicken and discard the vegetables. Add the rest of the cubed vegetables and simmer until tender.

Remove the skin and bones from the chicken and cut the meat into bite-size chunks. Reheat the chicken in the soup. Add the rest of the parsley and the dill and serve immediately in preheated bowls. Garnish with a stalk of dill.

GRANDMA'S CHICKEN SOUP

ICE HOCKEY IN ITALY

Federation

Registered Players:	6454
Senior:	1976
Juvenile:	4085
Female:	393

Referees

Male:	157
Female:	4

Rinks

Indoor:	53
Outdoor:	10

Participation

WM I, WW II, WM20 I, WM18 I

Population	58,126,212

ITALY

ITALY'S HOCKEY HISTORY

The country's first indoor ice rink opened in Milan on December 28, 1923. The Hockey Club Milano was soon playing ice hockey in the new arena. Italy's first hockey association was created in 1924, and was later admitted into the IIHF. Italy competed for the most part in the «B» Pool World Championship. They finished seventh in «A» Pool in 1933 and 1956 but slipped to «C» Pool six times from 1966–1979. Through most of the 1990s the squad maintained a place in «A» Pool including a sixth place finish as host in 1994. Their best finish at the Olympics was seventh place in 1956.

9 oz. cooked white beans

4 leaves savoy cabbage

1 Swiss chard

4 leaves black cabbage

1 leek

4 tomatoes (peeled, finely sliced)

1 medium potato (finely sliced)

1 onion (finely cut)

1 carrot (finely sliced)

1 zucchini (finely cubed)

5 oz. Italian bread

4 tbsp. extra virgin olive oil

Pepper and salt

Garnish

4 tbsp. parmesan (grated)

1 bn. parsley (finely chopped)

2 sprigs thyme (chopped)

4 basil leaves

Boil the white beans in sufficient water for 1 hour. In a separate soup pot, fry the onions in 2 tablespoons of olive oil at medium heat. Add the rest of the vegetables and simmer for 10 minutes. Add the beans including the water and simmer for another 2 hours.

Toast the bread and put it in the bottom of a soup bowl. Add the soup as well as the rest of the olive oil. Put the grated parmesan on top. Garnish with the herbs.

MINESTRONE
VEGETABLE SOUP

⬤ JAPAN

JAPAN'S HOCKEY HISTORY

Teams from Tokyo, Waseda, and Tomakomai founded the Japan Ice Hockey Federation in 1929. Japan became a member of the IIHF on January 26, 1930. In the aftermath of World War II, Japan was barred from the IIHF from 1946–1951. The Japanese competed in six consecutive Olympiads between 1960–1980. One of their best players during the 1960s was netminder Shoichi Tomita. To date, he still serves as Japan's representative on the IIHF Council. Japan hosted the 1972 Sapporo Olympics and finished ninth after defeating West Germany and Yugoslavia. Japanese goalie Yutaka Fukufuji made history in early 2007 when he played in a game for the Los Angeles Kings. He was the first Japanese player to appear in the NHL.

ICE HOCKEY IN JAPAN

Federation

Registered Players:	21027
Senior:	12335
Juvenile:	6951
Female:	1741

Referees

Male:	875
Female:	64

Rinks

Indoor:	125
Outdoor:	114

Participation

WM I, WW, WM20 II, WM18 I, WW18 I

Population	127,078,679

3 c. chicken stock

2 mushrooms
(shiitake or white button, thinly sliced)

1½ tbsp. miso paste

1 tbsp. Japanese soy sauce

1½ oz. "Silben" tofu (cut into cubes)

Garnish

½ scallion (thinly sliced on the diagonal)

1 heart of a celery stalk (finely chopped)

1 tomato (peeled, in strips)

Bring the stock to a gentle boil in a saucepan, add the mushrooms and simmer for 3 minutes. Mix together miso and soy sauce in a small bowl, then add to the hot stock. Add the tofu. Heat the soup and just before it comes to a boil remove from the heat. Pour the soup into bowls and garnish with the sliced scallions, celery and tomatoes.

MISO SOUP
WITH TOFU AND MUSHROOMS

KAZAKHSTAN

KAZAKHSTAN'S HOCKEY HISTORY

Hockey in Kazakhstan dates back to the 1950s when the first teams were created in what was then a Soviet Republic. The Kazakhstan Ice Hockey Federation was created as part of the Soviet Ice Hockey Federation in 1991 and became a separate organization when Kazakhstan gained its independence in 1992. In 1993, the national team made its World Championship debut, winning the bronze medal at the «C» Pool World Championship. Kazakhstan's first major upset took place when it stunned Canada in the fifth place game at the 1997 World U20 Championship. A few weeks later, at Nagano, the Olympic team earned respect by winning their preliminary round. Kazakhstan earned promotion to the elite Division in 2010.

ICE HOCKEY IN KAZAKHSTAN

Federation

Registered Players:	5251
Senior:	563
Juvenile:	4697
Female:	92

Referees

Male:	14
Female:	5

Rinks

Indoor:	10
Outdoor:	32

Participation
WM I, WW, WM20, WM18 I

Population	15,399,437

10 oz. yogurt

½ c. water

2 eggs (boiled)

1 green pepper

2 spring onions

1 cucumber (peeled)

1 tbsp. paprika

1 bn. parsley

1 bn. dill

1 bn. basil

2 sprigs thyme

Mix the yogurt and the water. Cut the herbs, the eggs and the cucumber in small pieces and mix with pepper, yogurt and water. Pureé mixture with a hand processor. Season to taste with paprika and salt.

SUMMER SOUP

KOREA

KOREA'S HOCKEY HISTORY

The earliest known hockey game in Korea took place in 1928, when the Yonsan Railway Club of Seoul faced the Tokyo University team. The members of this railway club organized informal matches and soon had a rival in the Kyungsung University team. The modern Korea Ice Hockey Association was founded in 1947. The country joined the IIHF on July 25, 1963. In 1965, the first IIHF-sanctioned match took place when a University team from Japan visited. The national team debuted with a seventh place finish at the 1979 «C» Pool World Championship. Korea are often too good for Division II, but they can't find a way to stay on the Division I level.

ICE HOCKEY IN KOREA

Federation

Registered Players:	1247
Senior:	97
Juvenile:	1052
Female:	98

Referees

Male:	39
Female:	6

Rinks

Indoor:	34
Outdoor:	4

Participation
WM II, WM20 II, WM18 II

Population	48,508,972

9 oz. beef steak

1 bn. soup vegetables
(e.g. carrots, root celery, leeks)

1 lb. beef soup meat

1 Korean radish

7 oz. Chinese noodles

1 large onion (chopped)

5 cloves garlic (pressed)

Salt and black pepper

Kimtchi (Korean pickled cabbage)

Cover the soup meat with cold water, add the soup vegetables and bring to a boil. Reduce the heat and cook gently for 1 hour or until the meat is tender. Remove the meat from the stock and set aside. Leave the stock to cool. After the stock is cold, remove the solidified fat from the surface of the stock. Chop the soup meat and the radish in strips and add to the stock. Add the garlic and onion to the stock and bring to a boil. Add the noodles and cook until tender.

Fry the beef steak on a high heat and cut it into slices. Put the soup in a bowl and serve the beef steak and Kimtchi on the side, each in its own dish.

BEEF NOODLE SOUP

KUWAIT'S HOCKEY HISTORY

Ice hockey in Kuwait became a reality in May, 2009, with a new league, governmental support and sponsorship. The following four clubs have been a member since its establishment: Qadsia Club, Kuwait Club, Kathma Club and Salmia Club. More clubs are expected to build their own hockey teams in the upcoming years. Ice hockey players and managers in Kuwait are excited to develop the game in their country on the national and international level, and are commited to being an active member of the IIHF.

Kuwait Ice Hockey Committee

KUWAIT

ICE HOCKEY IN KUWAIT

Federation
Registered Players:	306
Senior:	250
Juvenile:	60
Female:	56

Referees
Male:	3
Female:	0

Rinks
Indoor:	3
Outdoor:	0

Participation -

Population 2,691,158

2 c. lentils (washed)

1 onion (coarsely chopped)

2 cloves garlic (crushed)

5 c. water

1 tbsp. ghee

1 clove garlic (minced)

2 tsp. cumin

6 oz. (1 small can) tomato paste

3 dried lemons or loomi

8½ c. water

1 cup mini okra

Put the washed lentils with onion and garlic in a pot with the water. Let it boil, and wait until it dries up. Puree the lentils in a blender. In a pot, fry some garlic in some ghee, then add the cumin. Stir and add the tomato paste, then the puréed lentils. Add the second measure of water, the okra and the dried lemons. (If you want to make a stew, add less water and 2 peeled and cut potatoes at this stage). Let the mixture boil, then reduce the temperature and let it simmer on lower heat until done.

BAMIA SOUP

LATVIA

LATVIA'S HOCKEY HISTORY

The Latvian Ice Hockey Federation was founded on January 5, 1923, and became a member of the IIHF on February 22, 1931. The first well-known Latvian player was Helmut Balderis, who starred for the Soviet National Team from 1976–1983 Latvians Arturs Irbe and Sandis Ozolinsh made large impacts in the NHL during the 1990s. After re-gaining its independence following the breakup of the Soviet Union, Latvia rose quickly through the World Championship pool system. Latvia won the «C» Pool tournament in 1993, and the «B» Pool competition three years later. They finished 7th at their first «A» Pool World Championship in 1997. They have stayed with the elite nations since then and finished among the Top-8 teams four times. Latvia has been qualified to the 2002, 2006 and 2010 Olympic Winter Games.

ICE HOCKEY IN LATVIA

Federation

Registered Players:	4539
Senior:	2947
Juvenile:	1501
Female:	91

Referees

Male:	170
Female:	23

Rinks

Indoor:	18
Outdoor:	5

Participation

WM, WW II, WM20, WM18 I

Population   2,231,503

1 big red beet
(boiled, grated in chippings)

1 pt. sour milk
(alternatively use Greek yoghurt)

1 fresh cucumber (peeled, seeded, cubed)

1 pn. sugar

3 tbsp. sour cream

1 c. cold water

Salt

Garnish

2 egg yolks (cooked, mashed)

Spring onions (finely chopped)

4 sprigs dill (finely chopped)

½ lb. boiled new potatoes

Whip the sour milk. Add the water, the beets (lemon juice if beets are not pickled), cucumber, sugar, the sour cream. Salt to taste. Refrigerate until cold.

For the garnish mix the egg yolk and the spring onions. Serve the soup in a bowl top with the egg mix and the dill. Serve with boiled potatoes.

COLD BEET SOUP

LIECHTENSTEIN

LIECHTENSTEIN'S HOCKEY HISTORY

The Grand Duchy was admitted to the IIHF in 2001. Not having any indoor ice rink in the nation of around 33,000 inhabitants, the top club team EHC Vaduz-Schellenberg plays in the Swiss fourth Division. Four years after Liechtenstein joined the IIHF, the country listed over 100 players and on March 11, 2007, Liechtenstein played its first-ever national team game against Luxembourg, losing 4–2. The even score against Luxembourg which at that point was 43rd in the IIHF World Ranking and taking part in the Division III of the IIHF World Championship was an indication that Liechtenstein would soon be ready to join the IIHF World Championship program.

ICE HOCKEY IN LIECHTENSTEIN

Federation

Registered Players:	96
Senior:	69
Juvenile:	27
Female:	0

Referees

Male:	1
Female:	0

Rinks

Indoor:	0
Outdoor:	3

Participation	-
Population	34,761

10 oz. leeks (cut in rings)

1 tbsp. oil

2 tbsp. water

1½ oz. barley

2 ½ c. vegetable broth

Some full cream

Nutmeg

Lovage (celery seed)

Chives

Salt

Heat the oil in a pot and sauté the leeks. Add the water and then the barley. Thereafter, add the vegetable broth. Simmer for about 30 minutes.

To finish the soup, add a bit of full cream and the chives, lovage, salt and nutmeg, and season to taste. Optional: Add a bit of lemon juice to taste; however, leave out the cream as it will separate.

LEEK AND BARLEY SOUP

ICE HOCKEY IN LITHUANIA

Federation

Registered Players:	817
Senior:	278
Juvenile:	539
Female:	0

Referees

Male:	17
Female:	1

Rinks

Indoor:	5
Outdoor:	1

Participation

WM I, WM20 II, WM18 I

Population	3,555,179

LITHUANIA

LITHUANIA'S HOCKEY HISTORY

The Lithuanian Ice Hockey Federation was founded on October 14, 1932, and Lithuania joined the IIHF in 1932. It was expelled on April 26, 1946, after becoming a part of the Soviet Union. The newly independent Lithuania had its hockey federation reinstated in 1991, and rejoined the IIHF on May 6, 1992. The national team played its first game on February 27, 1932, a 3–0 loss to Latvia. Lithuania debuted at the World Championship in 1938, and beat Romania 1–0 for its only victory. The country played its last international game in Kaunus in 1941, suffering a 3–0 loss to Estonia. The Lithuanians returned to the world stage in 1995 at the «C» Pool World Championship where they finished 11th. Today, Lithuania is a regular in Division I.

7 oz. whole wheat bread
(in cubes, lightly roasted)

4 tbsp. honey

10 oz. seeded cherries or strawberries

1¼ c. water

Garnish

2 tbsp. whole wheat bread
(in cubes, lightly roasted)

Mix the water and honey well. Add the bread and the fruit, mixing well.

SUMMER BREAD SOUP

ICE HOCKEY IN LUXEMBOURG

Federation

Registered Players:	320
Senior:	150
Juvenile:	160
Female:	10

Referees

Male:	20
Female:	0

Rinks

Indoor:	2
Outdoor:	1

Participation
WM III

Population	491,775

LUXEMBOURG

LUXEMBOURG'S HOCKEY HISTORY

The Luxembourg Ice Hockey Federation is one of the oldest in Europe, formed in 1912. Luxembourg joined the IIHF on March 23, 1912, but hockey in the country grew slowly. Luxembourg did not hold its first national championship until 1978. The national team appeared on the international scene at the «C» Pool World Championship in 1992. The team lost its first game to South Africa 23–0. In 1998, Luxembourg iced a national junior team at the «D» Pool European Junior Championship. The Luxembourgian national ice hockey team represents the Grand Duchy of Luxembourg at ice hockey, and plays in Division III.

1 lb. green beans (1½-inch pieces)

1 lb. carrots (½-inch cubes)

1 lb. potatoes (½-inch cubes)

4 pt. bouillon

1 lb. bacon

4 Mettwurscht
(small smoked sausage, sliced)

Salt and pepper

Put the bouillon together with the cut vegetables and the bacon into a pan. Cover and simmer for 1 hour until everything is soft. Season to taste.

Meanwhile simmer the Mettwurscht in water for approx. ¼ hour in separate pot. Remove the Mettwurscht and the bacon and cut the Mettwurscht into slices and the bacon into ½-inch pieces. Put some meat into each preheated plate and add the soup.

BOUNESCHLUPP

ICE HOCKEY IN MALAYSIA

Federation

Registered Players:	250
Senior:	130
Juvenile:	88
Female:	20

Referees

Male:	5
Female:	0

Rinks

Indoor:	1
Outdoor:	0

Participation -

Population 25,715,819

MALAYSIA'S HOCKEY HISTORY

The Sunway Pyramid Ice Rink is the only hockey arena in Malaysia, and the Adun Subang Jaya ice hockey league represents the only formal hockey in the country. There have been four national championships in the country in 2001, 2002, 2005 and 2006.

MALAYSIA

1½-2 lbs. mutton, goat or lamb (in chunks, preferably bony cuts: shanks, ribs)

Paste of spices (recipe below)

2-3 tbsp. vegetable oil

1-2 tsp. sugar

6-8 c. water

2 tomatoes (quartered)

Salt and black pepper (freshly ground)

2 stalks scallions (chopped)

2 stalks Chinese celery
(or tender stalks of celery, chopped)

Paste

2 cloves garlic

1 cinnamon stick (2-inches, broken up)

4 cardamoms (smashed)

½-inch ginger (peeled)

8 black pepper corns

1 mace

2 big onions (diced)

3 bay leaves

Using a pestle and mortar, grind all the above ingredients into a smooth paste.

Heat vegetable oil in a hot wok or large frying pan, add brown mutton pieces in small portions and fry until brown and pores are closed. Set the meat aside. In a separate stockpot, heat vegetable oil, add ground paste, fry for about 5 minutes.

Add mutton, tomatoes, sugar, and water. Season with salt and freshly ground black pepper. Bring to a boil, cover, reduce heat to simmer, stirring occasionally, until mutton is very tender, for about 50 minutes to an hour. From time to time, skim off as much surface fat as possible. Ladle soup into individual soup bowls, garnish with scallions, celery and fried shallots. Serve hot as a starter, or as a main course with steamed rice.

Garnish
6-8 shallots
(thinly sliced, fried golden brown)

MUTTON SOUP

MEXICO

MEXICO'S HOCKEY HISTORY

The Federacion Mexicana de Deportes Invernales A.C. (Mexican Federation of Winter Sports) was founded in 1984. Mexico joined the IIHF the following year. At the time, Mexico boasted two indoor rinks—one in Mexico City and one in Guadalajara—along with six hockey teams. The first national championship was held in 1988–89, and was won by the Association del Estado de Mexico. Currently, there is no Mexican national championship. Mexico competed internationally for the first time in 1997, when the National Junior Team competed in the «D» Pool World Junior Championships. They returned to the same tourney the following year with somewhat improved results. Under the guidance of Canadian Daniel Gendron, the National Junior Team gained valuable experience in November 1997, when they toured part of Canada.

ICE HOCKEY IN MEXICO

Federation

Registered Players:	2220
Senior:	400
Juvenile:	1800
Female:	20

Referees

Male:	19
Female:	3

Rinks

Indoor:	18
Outdoor:	0

Participation
WM II, WM20 II, WM18 II

Population	111,211,789

2 tbsp. corn oil

1 red onion (finely chopped)

2 cloves garlic (pressed)

1 c. dry white wine

10 tomatoes (very ripe, seeded, cubed)

7 oz. sweet corn (canned, drained)

1 chili (seeded, finely chopped)

1 tsp. Indian caraway seeds (jeera)

1 pn. cayenne pepper

4 c. vegetable (or chicken) stock

1 tbsp. cilantro leaves (finely chopped)

Juice of 1 lime

Seasalt and pepper

Garnish

Cilantro leaves

1 ripe avocado (cubed)

2 slices of lime

2 wheat tortillas (cut)

Heat oil in a in a soup pan and glaze onions and garlic. Add the white wine and reduce until there is no more liquid. Add the tomatoes, sweet corn, chili, caraway seeds, and cayenne pepper and simmer for 10 minutes. Now add the stock and simmer gently for a further 20 minutes until the soup thickens slightly. Season to taste. Garnish with chopped cilantro leaves and lime juice. Serve immediately.

TOMATO AND TORTILLA SOUP

ICE HOCKEY IN MOLDOVA

Federation

Registered Players:	217
Senior:	68
Juvenile:	159
Female:	0
Referees	
Male:	0
Female:	0
Rinks	
Indoor:	2
Outdoor:	2
Participation	-
Population	4,320,740

MOLDOVA

MOLDOVA'S HOCKEY HISTORY

Moldova joined the IIHF as an associate member in 2008. Their two indoor rinks are located in the cities Chisinau and Tiraspol. Since its creation in May, 2007, the Moldovan Ice Hockey Federation has been building and maintaining close partnership relations with the national associations of its neighbouring countries and regularly participates in regional tournaments organized in the Ukraine, Russia, Latvia and Belarus.

1 soup chicken

1 onion (unpeeled, whole)

1 onion (peeled, whole)

3 carrots (sliced)

2 parsley roots

1 cayenne pepper

Herbs (bouquet of soup herbs)

1 cup of Kvass (fermented from old bread, alternatively few drops of lemon juice)

For the noodles

2 eggs

1-1½ c. flour (depends on size of eggs)

Garnish

Herbs (chopped)

Cut the chicken into portion pieces. Place the chicken pieces and 1 unpeeled onion in a pot with 6½ pints of water and simmer for 1½-2 hours. While the soup is simmering prepare the noodles. Mix eggs with flour and knead into a smooth, rather strong, but elastic, dough. Roll the dough into very thin sheets and cut the noodles. Then let them dry.

20 minutes before the soup is done, add the second onion, the carrots, a root of parsley and the herbs. Simmer until the carrots are tender. Remove the meat, the onions, the parsley root and the bouquet of herbs. Separate the meat from the bones and cut into bite-size pieces. Season the remaining broth with salt and pepper. Boil the noodles in a separate pot; then rinse the noodles well before adding the noodles to the broth. Add the meat and the Kvass to the soup to make it slightly sour. Boil again for 10 minutes. Serve the soup garnished with some chopped herbs and a spoon of sour cream and season with cayenne pepper.

ZAMA

MONGOLIA'S HOCKEY HISTORY

The history of Mongolian hockey started in the mid-60s when guest workers from ally Soviet Union introduced the game, mostly in the region around the capital Ulaanbaatar. They left some equipment behind and that was the start of Mongolian ice hockey. The Mongolian Ice Hockey Association was established on November 30, 1991. The Mongolian Hockey League was introduced in 1998. The country's governing body of ice hockey became an IIHF member in 1999, and in the same year, the national team participated in the Asian Winter Games. The first-ever Mongolian participation in an official IIHF event was at the 2000 IIHF Asia Oceanic U18 Championship Division II in Bangkok. Today, a Division III nation.

MONGOLIA

MONGOLIA

ICE HOCKEY IN MONGOLIA

Federation

Registered Players:	890
Senior:	390
Juvenile:	500
Female:	0

Referees

Male:	23
Female:	0

Rinks

Indoor:	0
Outdoor:	17

Participation
WM III, WM18 III

Population	3,041,142

1 lb. beef (cut in small pieces)

1 tbsp. flour

2 onions (chopped)

2 carrots (cut in rings)

1 knob butter

4 pt. meat stock

1 pn. seasoning

Salt

For the steamed flour

12 oz. flour

1 egg

Red oil

Garnish

1 spring onion (chopped)

Mix flour with egg, add a bit of salt water and knead to smooth dough. Roll the dough with the red oil (chili oil) and steam for 15 minutes. After steaming, cut into fine strips. Dust the cut beef in a tablespoon of flour and then fry the beef in half the butter. Remove from pan (keep the pan for later). Put the meat stock into a large pan, add the beef and simmer for 10-15 minutes. Heat the rest of the butter in the pan and fry the onions and carrots. Add the fried carrots and onions to the soup and season to taste. Place the strips of steamed dough into large bowls and add the soup. Garnish with chopped spring onions.

STEAMED FLOUR SOUP

ICE HOCKEY IN NAMIBIA*

Federation

Registered Players:	429
Senior:	43
Juvenile:	328
Female:	58

Referees

Male:	71
Female:	3

Rinks

Indoor:	4
Outdoor:	1

Participation	-
Population	2,108,665

*There is no ice hockey in Namibia. The above information refers to their Inline Hockey program.

NAMIBIA'S HOCKEY HISTORY

Namibia is one of the IIHF's newest members, joining the federation in 1998. To date, Namibia does not have any ice hockey activities within the country. Rather, inline hockey has started as an introduction of the sport. Considering Namibia's geographic location, a neighbour to South Africa which as a significant history in ice hockey, it is very possible that the sport can develop within its own borders in the near future.

NAMIBIA

1 tbsp. butter

2 onions (chopped into small pieces)

1 lb. butternut pumpkin

1 green apple (cubed)

2 tbsp. flour

1 tsp. curry powder (medium)

1 tsp. cumin (jeera)

3 c. chicken stock

1 c. milk

Juice of 1 orange

Peel of 1 orange (finely grated)

1 pn. sugar

Salt and pepper

Garnish

2 oz. whipped cream

4 sprigs parsley

Melt the butter in a pan and sauté the onions until light brown. Add the apple and the butternut and continue to sauté. Add the flour, curry powder and cumin and continue to simmer. Add the orange juice, grated peel, chicken stock and the milk and bring to a boil. Let simmer for 15 minutes until the butternut is tender. Pass the mixture through a strainer and puree the soup in a blender.

Place the soup in a clean pot and season to taste with salt, pepper and sugar. Just before serving add the whipped cream and place the soup in preheated bowls. Garnish with a small stalk of parsley.

BUTTERNUT SOUP

THE NETHERLANDS

THE NETHERLANDS' HOCKEY HISTORY

Hockey was not introduced in the Netherlands until the early 1930s. The country's first artificial ice rink was build in The Hague in 1937, though the first indoor arena did not appear until 1961 in Amsterdam. The Dutch Ice Hockey Union was founded on September 6, 1934, and the Netherlands joined the IIHF on January 20, 1935. The national team made its debut with a 4–0 loss to Belgium on January 5, 1935. Two weeks later, the Netherlands made its first appearance at the World and European Championships in Davos, Switzerland. The Netherlands lost their first game 6–0 to Hungary on January 19. The Dutch made their initial Olympic appearance when they tied for 9th place at the 1980 Lake Placid Games.

ICE HOCKEY IN THE NETHERLANDS

Federation

Registered Players:	3059
Senior:	1756
Juvenile:	1128
Female:	175

Referees

Male:	60
Female:	10

Rinks

Indoor:	21
Outdoor:	3

Participation
WM I, WW II, WM20 II, WM18 II

Population 16,715,999

1 lb. split peas

1 piece gammon with bone
(or about 1 lb. pork hock, or spareribs, or 2 pig's trotters)

3½ oz. streaky bacon or Dutch 'sauerkraut bacon' (streaky pork, salted but not smoked, preferably with rind)

1 smoked sausage

2 large onions (chopped not too small)

1 large carrot (finely cubed)

2 leeks

1 celery root (finely cubed)

2 potatoes (peeled and finely cubed)

1 bn. celery (finely chopped)

Pepper and salt

Bread or rye bread (pumpernickel)

Rinse the split peas in a sieve under the running tap. You do not need to let them soak in water. Bring water to the boil with the peas, gammon and bacon. Let it boil and skim off the floating scum. Pour off, rinse again and put peas and meat back on the fire with clean water.

Continue to simmer the peas and meat. Add the vegetables and let simmer until the peas are done (1½-2 hours—the split peas must be broken). Take the meat out of the pan, remove rind and bones, and cut it in small pieces. Put the meat back into the pan. Add the whole smoked sausage and the celery and cook for another 20 minutes. Season to taste. Just before serving, remove the sausage and cut into pieces. Serve the soup in preheated bowls with rye bread.

DUTCH PEA SOUP

NEW ZEALAND

NEW ZEALAND'S HOCKEY HISTORY

Ice hockey has been played in New Zealand for over 60 years. The first organized hockey tournament in New Zealand was held at Opawa near Albury in 1937. New Zealand became a member of the IIHF on May 2, 1977. The inaugural club competition for the Norm Hawker Shield was held at the Big Apple rink in Christchurch. The tournament featured ten teams and took place from June 19–21, 1987. Also in 1987, the national team made its debut in the «D» Pool World Championship. The first official game was on March 13, 1987, and resulted in a 35–2 loss to South Korea. The national team is today between Division II and Division III level.

ICE HOCKEY IN NEW ZEALAND

Federation

Registered Players:	1510
Senior:	800
Juvenile:	600
Female:	110

Referees

Male:	113
Female:	6

Rinks

Indoor:	6
Outdoor:	3

Participation

WM III, WM20 II, WM18 III

Population 4,213,418

⅔ c. butter

⅔ c. flour

7 c. milk

4 c. baking potatoes
(baked, cooled, peeled, cubed)

2 green onions (thinly sliced)

1 ¼ c. shredded mild cheddar cheese

1 c. sour cream

¾ tsp. salt

½ tsp. pepper

Garnish
12 strips bacon (fried, drained)

In a large stockpot over low heat, melt butter. Stir in flour until smooth and bubbly. Gradually add cold milk, stirring constantly to avoid lumps. Continue heating until sauce has thickened. Add potatoes and onions. Continue to cook, stirring constantly, until soup begins to bubble. Reduce heat, simmer gently for 10 minutes. Add remaining ingredients, stir until cheese is melted. Serve baked potato soup immediately. Garnish with bacon strips on top or crumble them and mix into the soup.

BAKED POTATO SOUP

NORWAY

NORWAY'S HOCKEY HISTORY

The first Norwegian national championship was played in 1934 and won by the Trygg SFK club of Oslo. That season also saw the formation of the Norwegian Ice Hockey Union on September 18, 1934, and the inclusion of Norway in the IIHF on January 20, 1935. The national team debuted on February 13, 1937, and was defeated 13–2 by Switzerland in the European Championship. However, Norway later won a bronze medal at the European Championship in 1951 and 1962. Norway played chiefly in «B» Pool from 1961–1991 but returned to «A» Pool through most of the 1990s. Norway is today one of the most improved national teams in the IIHF's program, finishing a strong 11th in the 2009 Worlds.

ICE HOCKEY IN NORWAY

Federation
Registered Players:	6385
Senior:	1993
Juvenile:	3934
Female:	458

Referees
Male:	141
Female:	14

Rinks
Indoor:	37
Outdoor:	3

Participation
WM, WW I, WM20 I, WM18, WW18 I

Population
	4,660,539

3 c. fish stock

12 oz. monkfish (in large cubes)

1 tbsp. butter

1 tbsp. wheat flour

1½ tbsp. vinegar

1½ tbsp. sugar

½ c. double cream

½ c. sour cream

Salt and pepper

Garnish

1 carrot (juliennes)

1 leek (juliennes, blanched)

Chives (finely chopped)

A little bit of fresh thyme

In a large pan, melt the butter. Add the flour, stirring continuously (low heat). Add the fish stock and stir continuously until the flour has completely dissolved. Bring to a boil and cook for 10 minutes. Add the double cream, vinegar and sugar. Salt and pepper to taste. The soup should taste a little bit sweet and sour. Turn off the heat and once the soup has stopped cooking whip in the sour cream. Add the fish cubes, wait a few minutes until fish is warm (do not cook!) and place the soup in bowls.

Garnish with the blanched leek and carrot julienne. Top it off with the chives and the thyme.

FISH SOUP
FROM BERGEN

ICE HOCKEY IN POLAND

Federation

Registered Players:	2923
Senior:	559
Juvenile:	1136
Female:	228

Referees

Male:	78
Female:	1

Rinks

Indoor:	21
Outdoor:	7

Participation

WM I, WM20 I, WM18 I

Population	38,482,919

POLAND

POLAND'S HOCKEY HISTORY

Four clubs in Warsaw established the Polish Ice Hockey Union in January of 1925. The PZHL joined the IIHF on January 11, 1926. Six teams participated in the first Polish national championship in 1927. Poland first participated in international tournaments in 1926 and has been entering the World Championships ever since. Polish hockey flourished during the late 1920s and early 1930s, but was slow to recover after World War II. The construction of the country's first indoor ice rinks in the early 1950s helped rekindle the game. The national team played at the World Championship «A» Pool level in the 1950s but slipped to «B» Pool in 1961. Since that time, Poland has alternated between these two levels, today most of the time in Division I.

5 oz. pearl barley

1 c. dried mushrooms

1 carrot

1 celery root

1 leek

1 onion

Several dill sprigs

2 tbsp. parsley leaves (chopped)

1 tbsp. spring onions (chopped)

5 tbsp. frozen green beans (or peas)

Garnish

6 tbsp. sour cream

1 tbsp. butter

1 parsley root

Place mushrooms in bowl and dowse with 2 cups boiling water. Let them soak for 20 minutes. Drain the mushrooms, collecting the juice to be used later. Press the rest of the water out of the mushrooms.

Glaze the barley with the butter. Add the vegetables, mushrooms, salt and dill and simmer. Add the mushroom juice and add water to bring up to about 3 pints of liquid. Let simmer until the barley is soft. Add the beans at the very end and cook in the soup until tender.

Glaze the cut parsley in a spoon of butter. Add to the sour cream and blend. Serve the soup in a bowl garnished with the parsley cream.

MUSHROOM SOUP
WITH PEARL BARLEY

PORTUGAL

PORTUGAL'S HOCKEY HISTORY

The Portuguese Ice Sports Federation was founded in 1998, with Portugal having been the last of the western-European countries to become a member of the IIHF. Unfortunately, the sport is challenged in Portugal by mild winters without natural ice. Despite the lack of appropriate infrastructure for ice hockey (only one artificial ice rink), the federation organized in-Portugal tournaments with teams from Spain, Finland, and Canada. Portuguese teams have taken part in tournaments in Spain and Turkey. Portugal is also active in inline hockey with one of their highlights being the participation of their national team at the 2005 IIHF Inline Hockey World Championships. To date, the Portuguese Federation cooperates with the inline hockey school OK Mania teaching the game to more than 200 children per season.

FPDG Federação Portuguesa de Desportos no Gelo

ICE HOCKEY IN PORTUGAL

Federation

Registered Players:	116
Senior:	48
Juvenile:	50
Female:	18
Referees	
Male:	5
Female:	2
Rinks	
Indoor:	1
Outdoor:	0
Participation	-
Population	10,707,924

½ lb. cabbage (chopped in fine strips)

21 oz. potatoes (diced)

4 cloves of garlic (finely chopped)

1 onion (finely diced)

2 Portuguese sausages *chouriço*

½ c. olive oil

Salt

Wash and drain the cabbage. Gently heat one quart of salt water in a stock pan. When the water reaches the boiling point, add the potatoes, garlic and onions. When all of the ingredients are well cooked, blend the soup. Bring the soup back to a boil.

Add the cabbage and the chouriço in thin slices. When the cabbage and the chouriço are cooked, add olive oil and stir for a few minutes. Ideally serve in an earthen ware bowl accompanied by corn bread.

CALDO VERDE

ROMANIA

ROMANIA'S HOCKEY HISTORY

In 1921, ice hockey began in Romania when the first games took place in Miercurea Cuic. The popularity of the game grew quickly, and in 1924, the Romania Ice Hockey Association was founded. On January 24, 1924, Romania joined the IIHF. Romania made its international debut at the World and European Championship in 1931. In the aftermath of a poor showing, the national team withdrew from international hockey for more than a decade. Romania has played chiefly in «B» and «C» pool since the 1960s. Their high point came when they qualified for «A» Pool in 1977. Today, Romania is back and forth between Division I and II.

ICE HOCKEY IN ROMANIA

Federation

Registered Players:	1500
Senior:	325
Juvenile:	1100
Female:	75

Referees

Male:	65
Female:	9

Rinks

Indoor:	5
Outdoor:	7

Participation

WM I, WM20 II, WM18 II

Population   22,215,421

8 oz. bacon (sliced)

2 onions (sliced)

2 green bell peppers (peeled, chopped)

1 cabbage (cut into slices)

Several sprigs dill and savory (chopped)

1½ qt. water

2 egg yolks

½ c. heavy cream (sweet or sour)

1 tsp. vinegar

Salt and pepper

Chop up and fry one slice of bacon until the fat runs. Fry the onions in the fat until golden. Add peppers and fry. Remove from heat. Layer the cabbage and the rest of the bacon into the soup pot. Season the layers with salt, pepper, and the herbs. Pour the water over it all and bring to a boil. Turn heat down and simmer for 40-50 minutes until vegetables are tender. Remove soup from the heat.

Beat the egg yolks with the cream and vinegar in a bowl. Stir in a ladleful of the hot soup. Whisk well, pour the mix into the soup to thicken and enrich. Serve in deep bowls accompanied with fresh bread.

CABBAGE SOUP
WITH BACON

ICE HOCKEY IN RUSSIA

Federation

Registered Players:	84720
Senior:	26185
Juvenile:	58257
Female:	278

Referees

Male:	523
Female:	11

Rinks

Indoor:	257
Outdoor:	3

Participation

WM, WW, WM20, WM18, WW18

Population 140,041,247

RUSSIA

RUSSIA'S HOCKEY HISTORY

The first official Soviet championship began on December 22, 1946, but a major turning point in Soviet hockey occurred in February of 1948 with the historic visit of the LTC Prague team of Czechoslovakia. Almost every player on the Prague team had been a member of the Czechoslovak squad which had received a silver medal at the St. Moritz Olympics. The results of the three-game series surprised many as the Moscow Selects won 6–3, lost 5–3, and tied 2–2. Even more startling was the success of the Soviet National Team when it entered the World Championship for the first time in 1954. The USSR defeated Canada 7–2 in the gold medal game in a contest that permanently altered the complexion of international hockey. Russian hockey enjoys today the best post-Soviet period with gold medals both in 2008 and 2009 and top world ranking.

5 oz. salmon filet

5 oz. pikeperch filet with skin

4 oz. monkfish

4 tiger prawns

2 pt. fish stock

1 onion (chopped)

1 tbsp. butter

1 tbsp. plain flour

3½ oz. cooked sauerkraut

2 oz. root vegetables (finely diced)

2 oz. celery root (finely chopped)

10 black olives (in ½)

2 pickled cucumbers (finely diced)

2 tbsp. juice of the pickled cucumbers

1 bay leaf

Salt and pepper

Garnish

1 bn. dill (finely chopped)

½ c. sour cream

1 pn. chili powder

Cut the fish filets in bite-size pieces. Glaze the onions in the butter in a stock pan. Add the fish stock, the root vegetables, sauerkraut and the bay leaf. Cook at a medium heat for 30 minutes. Season with salt and pepper. Add the fish, turn the heat off and wait until the fish is done. Shortly before serving add the pickled cucumbers, their juice and the olives. Mix the sour cream with the dill and the chili and salt to taste. Serve the soup in a warmed plate and garnish with the spiced sour cream.

SOLJANKA
FISH SOUP WITH CABBAGE

SERBIA

SERBIA'S HOCKEY HISTORY

The roots of ice hockey in Yugoslavia go back to 1906, when the first hockey team in Yugoslavia was formed in Zagreb. In 1930, the Yugoslav Ice Hockey Federation was founded and the country's first IIHF World Championship was in 1939. Yugoslavia had its strongest period in the late 60s and early 70s when the national team finished 9th at the 1968 Olympics and placed 8th (2nd in «B» Pool) in the 1974 IIHF World Championship. Yugoslavia competed under the old name until 2004, when it changed the name to Serbia and Montenegro. In 2006, Montenegro gained independence, and the country continued its IIHF membership as Serbia, where the game is basically centred around the capital Belgrade and the city of Novi Sad.

ICE HOCKEY IN SERBIA

Federation

Registered Players:	563
Senior:	191
Juvenile:	369
Female:	3

Referees

Male:	21
Female:	2

Rinks

Indoor:	3
Outdoor:	1

Participation

WM II, WM20 III, WM18 III

Population   7,379,339

½ lb. bacon (cut in cubes)

Bacon rind

2 cloves garlic (finely chopped)

A little celery root (diced)

3 onions

2 red peppers

7 oz. white beans (soaked)

Chili powder

Tomato paste

Pepper and salt

Boil the beans with the bacon rind in one quart of water for 45 minutes. Remove the bacon rind. Fry the bacon cubes in a frying pan without oil. Add the chopped onions, peppers and the chopped garlic, frying until everything is soft. Add the white beans with the water and the tomato paste. Let it simmer for about 20 minutes. Then press the white beans against the side of the pan as much as possible. Add some fresh celery and let the soup boil for another 10 minutes. Add pepper, salt and chili powder to taste.

WHITE BEAN SOUP

SINGAPORE

SINGAPORE'S HOCKEY HISTORY

The first hockey games in Singapore were played in the 1970s. Singapore joined the IIHF in 1996, but has not yet debuted at IIHF tournaments. It was not until 1988 that a rink was built in Singapore. In the mid-1990s the Fuji Ice Palace found a new location at Jurong East Entertainment Center where it is still in operation. It is the only operational ice skating rink in Singapore. In 1997, a local league was started at Fuji, organized by the Ice Hockey Association, Singapore with six teams. Between that time and the formation of the AIHA and NIHL in late 2000, pick-up sessions of informal games were organized by players. The Canadian Association of Singapore also runs hockey activities, most recently a comprehensive youth hockey program since 2001.

ICE HOCKEY IN SINGAPORE

Federation

Registered Players:	351
Senior:	185
Juvenile:	157
Female:	9

Referees

Male:	25
Female:	1

Rinks

Indoor:	1
Outdoor:	0
Participation	-
Population	4,657,542

2 spring onions (roughly chopped)

3-4 small green and red chilis (seeded, cut)

1½ cups chicken (or fish) stock

1 inch galangal root (thinly sliced)

2 lemon grass shoots (roughly chopped)

3 kaffir lime leaves (in broad strips)

2 coriander roots (cracked)

2 tbsp. rice

1 c. coconut cream

4 tiger prawns (peeled, cut into pieces)

7 oz. white button mushrooms (quartered)

3 cherry tomatoes (quartered)

4 oz. snow peas (finely chopped)

10 small Thai leeks (finely chopped)

1 tbsp. fish sauce

Juice of 2 limes

1 tsp. sugar

Garnish

Leaves of ½ bn. coriander

1 tsp. spicy chili oil

4 prawns with tail
(peeled, lightly sautéed in sesame seed oil)

4 lemon grass sticks (used as skewers)

Crush the spring onions and chilis with a pestle and mortar (the longer the spicier). Heat the chicken stock. When hot, blanch the prawns and the mushrooms. Remove with a skimming ladle, drip dry and set aside. Add the crushed onions and chilis, galangal, lemongrass, kaffir lime leaves and the rice to the stock and simmer for 20 minutes. Thereafter, sieve the stock and return to the pan. Add the coconut cream and simmer gently for 5 minutes. Add the blanched prawns, mushrooms and the cherry tomatoes, snow peas and Thai leeks. While stirring continuously simmer for a maximum 3–4 minutes. Round off the soup with fish sauce, lime juice and sugar. Take the remaining prawns with the tail on, sauté lightly in the sesame seed oil and put them individually on a lemongrass stick. Serve soup in a bowl, place the lemon grass prawn skewer on top and garnish the soup with coriander and chili oil.

COCONUT CREAM SOUP

ICE HOCKEY IN SLOVAKIA

Federation

Registered Players:	8671
Senior:	1886
Juvenile:	6497
Female:	288

Referees

Male:	368
Female:	21

Rinks

Indoor:	45
Outdoor:	21

Participation

WM, WW I, WM20, WM18, WW18 I

Population   5,463,046

SLOVAKIA

SLOVAKIA'S HOCKEY HISTORY

Hockey became popular after the 1925 European Championship was held in Stary Smokovec and won by the host country. In 1930, the Slovak Hockey Union organized its first official competition, the Slovak National Championship. After World War II, the Slovak clubs began shifting into the Czechoslovakian League. Three of these teams became national champions: Slovan Bratislava (1979), VSZ Kosice (1986 and 1988) and Dukla Trencin (1992). Shortly after the separation of Czechoslovakia into two independent countries in 1993, Slovakia qualified for its first Olympics. The Slovaks finished in a respectable sixth place. Later that year, Slovakia made its debut at the World Championship in the «C» Pool. Within two years they earned promotion to the «A» Pool. Within only a few years of independent existence as a young nation it would mark its biggest triumph ever by winning the World Championship in Sweden in 2002.

2 pt. meat stock

5 large potatoes
(peeled, roughly chopped)

Mushrooms (dry or fresh: if dry, let them
soak until soft, discard the water)

1 onion (peeled, chopped)

2 cloves of garlic (peeled, chopped)

3 bay leaves

½ pt. sour cream

1 bn. parsley

Oil

Salt and pepper (freshly ground)

Sugar

Boil the potatoes in salted water together with 3 bay leaves until they are cooked. Heat the oil in a pan and glaze the onions. Add the mushrooms and season with salt and pepper. After the mushrooms start to soften, add the garlic.

When the potatoes are ready, pick out the bay leaves, and pureé the potatoes with a hand mixer. If the soup is too thick, add some more meat stock. Add the mushrooms, a touch of sugar as well as the parsley. Stir thoroughly and then add the sour cream.

POTATO SOUP
WITH MUSHROOMS

SLOVENIA

SLOVENIA'S HOCKEY HISTORY

Hockey in Slovenia began on February 7, 1929, when the new hockey section of the Ilirija Sports Club in Ljubljana played against a team from Kamnik. Credit for introducing hockey to Slovenia is given to Stanko Bloudek, who brought the first hockey equipment to Ljubljana from Vienna in 1928. The Ice Hockey Federation of Slovenia was founded in 1991, and the newly independent nation of Slovenia joined the IIHF on May 6, 1992. Slovenia held its first national championship that year, and the national team played its first international game on March 20, 1992. Slovenia debuted in the top pool in 2002 and had returned to the Top 16 on four occasions.

ICE HOCKEY IN SLOVENIA

Federation

Registered Players:	1435
Senior:	902
Juvenile:	447
Female:	85

Referees

Male:	45
Female:	4

Rinks

Indoor:	8
Outdoor:	2

Participation

WM I, WM20 I, WM18 II

Population	2,005,692

2 lbs. beef (on the bone)

1 soup bone (with marrow)

4 pt. cold water

3 carrots (in cubes)

3 stalks of celery with leaves (finely chopped)

1 onion

2 cloves of garlic

1 bay leaf

8 black pepper corns (crushed)

Salt

Garnish

1 bn. parsley (finely chopped)

1 carrot (small cubes)

1 stalk of celery with leaves (finely chopped)

Bring the water to a boil, add the meat, and bring to a boil again. Remove the scum. Add all the stock ingredients and simmer for 1-2 hours. Remove the meat and the bone and pass the stock through a muslin cloth into a clean pan. Slice the meat and return to the stock. Add the other soup additions and simmer for 10 minutes. After serving, garnish with parsley, celery and carrots.

SLOVENIAN BEEF SOUP

SOUTH AFRICA

SOUTH AFRICA'S HOCKEY HISTORY

The South African Ice Hockey Association was founded in 1936, and became a member of the IIHF on February 25, 1937. South Africa played its first official game at the «C» Pool World Championship on March 3, 1961, when they dropped a 12–3 decision to Yugoslavia. They finished fifth at this tournament and did not reappear until their third place finish in 1966. Political sanctions against South Africa's apartheid policies left the country out of international hockey until the 1990s. After experiencing difficulties in «C» Pool from 1992–1995, South Africa withdrew for two years. They reemerged in 1998 as hosts of the «D» Pool World Championship.

ICE HOCKEY IN SOUTH AFRICA

Federation

Registered Players:	341
Senior:	129
Juvenile:	168
Female:	448

Referees

Male:	6
Female:	2

Rinks

Indoor:	4
Outdoor:	0

Participation
WM II, WM18 III

Population	49,052,489

1 lb. crayfish tails (rock lobster in USA)

1 tsp. salt

2 oz. butter

1 c. onions (thinly sliced)

2 tomatoes (chopped)

1 clove garlic (chopped)

1 tsp. salad herbs (finely chopped)

½ tsp. nutmeg

1 tsp. salt

½ tsp. pepper

Grated rind of 1 lemon

1 c. dry white wine

½ c. single cream

Boil 1¼ quarts of water in a large saucepan. Add the lobster tails and salt, and gently cook until tender. Take the lobster tails out of the water and remove the meat from the shells. Coarsely chop the meat and set aside. Reserve the stock.

In a separate large saucepan, heat the butter and sauté the onions for 5 minutes. Add the tomatoes, garlic, herbs, nutmeg, salt, pepper, and the grated lemon rind. Cook over low heat for 10 minutes. Add the wine and 4 cups lobster water. Boil soup and cook for a further 10 minutes. Blend the soup and return to the pot. Reheat the soup. Place the chopped lobster meat in a warmed soup bowl and pour the soup over it.

CRAYFISH SOUP

 # SPAIN

SPAIN'S HOCKEY HISTORY

Spain's first indoor rink with artificial ice was built in Madrid in the 1930s. The Spanish Winter Sports Federation was founded in 1923. On March 10 of that year, Spain joined the IIHF. The country participated in the 1924 European Championship, but lost 12–0 to Switzerland in its first international game. Over the next 25 years, ice hockey was rarely played in Spain. In 1986, the national team ceased operations. It returned to the «D» Pool championships in 1989. They played in «C» Pool from 1992–1995. Since then, Spain has played mostly in Division III.

ICE HOCKEY IN SPAIN

Federation

Registered Players:	780
Senior:	209
Juvenile:	438
Female:	133

Referees

Male:	25
Female:	1

Rinks

Indoor:	18
Outdoor:	0

Participation
WM II, WM20 II, WM18 II

Population 40,525,002

6 ramata tomatoes (peeled, finely cubed)

1 red bell pepper (hulled, finely chopped)

1 clove garlic (pressed)

1 small red onion (finely chopped)

1 chili pepper
(seeded, finely chopped)

1 c. vegetable stock

1 tbsp. red vine vinegar

2 tbsp. virgin olive oil

½ c. tomato juice

Salt and pepper (freshly ground)

1 tbsp. sea salt

1 pn. sugar

2 slices toast bread (without the crust)

Put all ingredients into a blender and mix well. Prior to serving cool for at least 2 hours and season to taste. Garlic croutons, chopped red onions, finely cut red bell peppers, finely cubed cucumber and/or a small chopped chili can be added to the soup.

GAZPACHO
COLD TOMATO SOUP

SWEDEN

SWEDEN'S HOCKEY HISTORY

On November 17, 1922, seven teams from Stockholm founded the Swedish Ice Hockey Union. National championships have been held in Sweden since 1922. The first artificial ice rink in Sweden was built in an airplane hangar in 1931, and it remained the country's only indoor arena until 1938, hosting 1,032 games over that time. The Swedish Ice Hockey Union was instrumental in making hockey one of the most popular sports in the country. Over the years, the national team has come to be known as Tre Kronor (Three Crowns) for the emblem on its uniform. To date, Sweden has won the World Championship in 1953, 1957, 1962, 1987, 1991, 1992 and 1998 and won an Olympic gold medal in 1994 and 2006.

ICE HOCKEY IN SWEDEN

Federation

Registered Players:	60374
Senior:	15685
Juvenile:	41104
Female:	3612

Referees

Male:	1984
Female:	40

Rinks

Indoor:	327
Outdoor:	136

Participation

WM, WW, WM20, WM18, WW18

Population	9,059,651

40-50 live mussels

1 onion (in rings)

1 bay leaf

1 large leek (only the white, chopped in rings)

2 tbsp. oil

2 tbsp. rice

2 pt. water

Salt

1 pn. saffron

Garnish

Parsley

Dill

Clean and wash the mussels. Place them in a stock pot together with the onions, bay leaf and 1 cup of boiling water. Place a well closing lid on the pan and cook until all mussels are open (approximately 4 minutes). When they are ready, remove with a skimming ladle. Sieve the mussel soup and set aside. Remove mussels from their shells and place them, covered, in a plate to protect them from drying.

Gently sauté the leek in the oil. Add the mussel stock carefully (ensuring all sand is left behind). Add the rice, saffron and 3 cups of water. Cook for 25 minutes. Turn off the heat. When the soup is no longer boiling, add the mussels (the mussels must not cook, otherwise they become rubbery). Season the soup to taste. Serve hot and garnish with parsley and dill.

MUSSEL SOUP

SWITZERLAND

SWITZERLAND'S HOCKEY HISTORY

Switzerland took part in Europe's first international hockey tournament at Chamonix, France in 1909. A 3–0 loss to tournament champion Great Britain represented the debut of the Swiss National Team. A year later, Switzerland hosted the first official European Championship with games on a frozen lake near Montreux. The Swiss claimed European titles in 1935, 1939 and 1950 along with a silver medal at the 1935 World Championship and bronze medals at the 1928 and 1948 Olympics. The Swiss remained a constant in the top level of World Championship competition until the 1950s. Between 1950 and 1991, the Swiss competed chiefly in «B» Pool with the odd excursion into «A» and «C» Pools. During the early 1990s they finished as high as fourth during the 1992 «A» Pool championship, a feat they repeated in 1998. The program has steadily improved under coach Ralph Krueger and today Switzerland ranks 7th in the world.

ICE HOCKEY IN SWITZERLAND

Federation

Registered Players:	24705
Senior:	10259
Juvenile:	13709
Female:	735

Referees

Male:	792
Female:	45

Rinks

Indoor:	157
Outdoor:	31

Participation
WM, WW, WM20 I, WM18, WW18

Population	7,604,467

3 oz. pearl barley

½ celery root (finely diced)

2 carrots (finely diced)

2 potatoes (finely diced)

½ white cabbage (finely chopped)

1 leek (cut into fine rings)

1 tbsp. oil

1 cube stock

10 oz. ham (or air-dried Grisons meat)

2 tbsp. cream

Salt and pepper (freshly ground)

Wash the barley and soak it overnight. Discard water. Boil 2½ quarts of water and add the stock cube. Add the barley and all vegetables and cook for 2½ hours. Add the ham and cook for a further 30 minutes. Salt and pepper to taste. Before serving, add the cream.

GRISONS BARLEY SOUP

TURKEY

TURKEY'S HOCKEY HISTORY

The first ice hockey rinks in Turkey were built in the 80s in Ankara and Istanbul. The Turkish Ice Sports Federation was created in 1991. In May of that year, Turkey became a member of the IIHF. The national team made its debut at the 1992 «C» Pool World Championship. In 1995, Turkey's national junior team debuted at the «C» Pool of the European Junior Championship. In 1997–98, the national team played in the «D» Pool at the World Championship.

ICE HOCKEY IN TURKEY

Federation

Registered Players:	790
Senior:	310
Juvenile:	320
Female:	160

Referees

Male:	75
Female:	10

Rinks

Indoor:	2
Outdoor:	0

Participation

WM III, WM20 III, WM18 III

Population	76,805,524

6 tbsp. butter

1 lb. lamb or beef (finely diced or ground)

1 carrot (finely chopped)

1 onion (finely chopped)

5 c. beef stock

2 egg yolks

Juice of ½ lemon

For the paprika butter

1 tbsp. butter

½ tbsp. paprika

Cayenne pepper

Garnish

Dusting of cinnamon

Melt the butter in a large saucepan, add meat, carrots, and onions and sauté over low heat for 10 minutes. Stir in flour and cook until blended. Gradually stir in stock, making sure nothing sticks to the bottom of the pan. Bring to a boil, then lower heat and simmer for an hour. Season to taste with salt, pepper and lemon juice.

Sauté the paprika and cayenne in a tablespoon of butter. Leave in hot pan. Now ladle the soup into preheated bowls and distribute the paprika mix equally into the bowls. Just before serving, carefully place in each bowl a whole egg yolk. Lightly dust the top of each bowl with cinnamon.

WEDDING SOUP

UKRAINE

UKRAINE'S HOCKEY HISTORY

Before the breakup of the Soviet Union, the Ukrainian Ice Hockey Federation was part of the Soviet Ice Hockey Federation. It became an independent federation in 1992, and joined the IIHF in May of that year. The Ukrainian national team made its debut on April 13, 1992, tying the Russian National B Team 3–3. The Ukraine made its first appearance at the World Championships at the «C» Pool tournament in 1993, soon after they earned promotion to the «B» Pool. The following year, the Ukraine continued its rise by winning the «B» Pool. This triumph qualified them for the «A» Pool. The first Ukrainian player to reach the NHL was Alexander Godynyuk.

ICE HOCKEY IN THE UKRAINE

Federation

Registered Players:	4228
Senior:	670
Juvenile:	3546
Female:	12

Referees

Male:	70
Female:	0

Rinks

Indoor:	20
Outdoor:	11

Participation
WM I, WM20 I, WM18 I

Population	45,700,395

1 lb. soup beef

2 bn. soup vegetables
(e.g. carrot, celery root, leek)

1 beetroot (finely chopped, in strips)

3½ oz. fresh white cabbage (finely chopped)

2 potatoes (finely diced)

2 carrots (finely diced)

1 parsley root (finely diced)

2 onions (finely chopped)

2 cloves garlic (peeled, pressed)

1 tbsp. tomato paste

½ red sweet pepper (finely chopped)

1 tbsp. melted butter

1 tsp. sugar

1 tbsp. fruit vinegar

2 parsley stalks (finely chopped)

Dill (finely chopped)

1 bay leaf

1 red hot chili

Salt

Garnish

1 c. sour cream

To prepare the stock, place the meat in a pan. Cover with cold water and bring to a boil. Skim the foam. Reduce the heat and cook until the meat is tender. Skim from time to time. When the meat is tender, remove it from the stock and set both aside.

Take a separate pan and warm the butter. Add the beetroot, the vinegar, sugar and the salt and sauté lightly. Then add the rest of the diced vegetables. Continue to sauté. Add the chili and the bay leaf. Mix the tomato paste with a small amount of stock and add the mixture to the sautéed vegetables. Cook for a further 10-15 minutes.

Remove the fat from the soup meat and cut the meat into small strips. Add it to the vegetables and add the stock. Bring to a boil and season with salt and pepper. Before serving, add the dill and parsley. Serve in a warmed bowl and garnish with sour cream.

UKRAINIAN BORSHCH

THE UNITED ARAB EMIRATES' HOCKEY HISTORY

The first hockey games were played in the United Arab Emirates (UAE) in the 1970s. The first national league was formed in 1979. The UAE Ice Hockey Committee was founded in 1998. UAE has not participated at a World Championship, but the national team has played at other international events. New clubs continued to emerge, with fourteen by 2001. During the 1999 Asian Hong Kong International Ice Hockey Cup, UAE claimed the title during their first ever international competition.

UNITED ARAB EMIRATES

ICE HOCKEY IN THE UNITED ARAB EMIRATES

Federation

Registered Players:	200
Senior:	80
Juvenile:	110
Female:	10

Referees

Male:	7
Female:	0

Rinks

Indoor:	4
Outdoor:	0

Participation -

Population 4,798,491

1 c. fine crushed grain (Jareesh)

1 lb. beef (or lamb) meat (chopped)

2 pt. water

1 lb. small tomatoes (in ½)

2 cloves garlic (crushed)

1 tbsp. oil

1 tbsp. instant vegetable broth

1 tbsp. cumin (jeera)

1 tsp. chili powder

1 tsp. crushed pepper

Salt

Garnish

Flat bread

Place oil, tomatoes and onions in a pot and fry at medium heat. Add some salt, instant vegetable broth and all spices and stew for 5 minutes until the soup thickens. Add the water, the meat and the wheat and simmer on low heat for 2½ hours. If needed, add some water. Salt to taste. Serve hot with Arabic flat bread (Khoubiz).

JAREESH

UNITED STATES OF AMERICA

USA'S HOCKEY HISTORY

The United States did not meet teams from outside North America until 1920. That year, the Americans made their international debut at the Olympics. In 1924–25, the Boston Bruins became the first US-based team in the National Hockey League. USA upset Canada in 1933 to win its first and only World Championship in a non-Olympic year. The U.S. won a surprising silver medal at the 1972 Olympics with a team that included Mark Howe and Robbie Ftorek on its roster, but the late 1960s and 1970s were not a good time for American hockey. In 1969, the United States sent more men to the moon than it did to the National Hockey League. But the nation rebounded with the now infamous 1980 Miracle on Ice, which cemented its place among the elite nations for future generations.

ICE HOCKEY IN THE USA

Federation
Registered Players:	465975
Senior:	112778
Juvenile:	293691
Female:	59506

Referees
Male:	25536
Female:	1330

Rinks
Indoor:	1800
Outdoor:	250

Participation
WM, WW, WM20, WM18, WW18

Population 307,212,123

2 tbsp. butter

1 medium-sized onion (chopped)

1 small carrot (peeled, finely diced)

2 tbsp. plain flour

2 lbs. fresh tomatoes
(peeled, seeded, chopped)

2 c. chicken broth
(reduced-sodium, canned)

1 tbsp. tomato paste

1 tbsp. fresh basil (or ½ tsp. dried basil)

2 tbsp. fresh thyme
(or ½ tsp. dried thyme leaves)

1 bay leaf

1 c. single cream (or milk)

Salt and pepper

In a large saucepan, melt butter over medium heat. Add onion and carrot and cook, stirring frequently, until softened, 3-5 minutes. Add flour and cook, stirring constantly, 1-2 minutes without allowing to colour. Add tomatoes with their juice, broth, tomato paste, basil, thyme and bay leaf. Bring to a boil. Reduce heat to low, cover, and simmer stirring frequently for 15 minutes. Remove and discard bay leaf.

In a food processor or blender, purée soup in batches until smooth. Return to pan and stir in the cream. Season with salt and pepper. Cook for a further 3-5 minutes and garnish with hot foamed milk or whipped cream.

CREAM OF TOMATO SOUP